THE BETRAYAL OF
THE WEST

THE BETRAYAL
OF THE WEST

Jacques Ellul

Translated by Matthew J. O'Connell

A Continuum Book
THE SEABURY PRESS · NEW YORK

1978
The Seabury Press
815 Second Avenue
New York, N.Y. 10017

Originally published as *Trahison de l'Occident* © Calmann-Lévy, 1975

Printed in the United States of America

Library of Congress Cataloging in Publication Data

Ellul, Jacques.   The betrayal of the West.
(A Continuum book)
Translation of Trahison de l'Occident.
Includes bibliographical references.
1. Civilization, Occidental. 2. Civilization,
Modern—1950–   I. Title.
CB245.E513   909′.09′821   77–26796
ISBN 0–8164–9338–3

CONTENTS

PROLOGUE

It is not clear what there is still to say about the West, after Massis, Spengler, Sombart, Dandieu, Ortega y Gasset, Malraux, and others have meditated on the greatness and decline of western civilization or have spoken out in its defense.

Not everything has been said, however. In this critical time when our civilization is being challenged, rejected without due consideration, and condemned with arguments that are not all bad, but with no one to plead in its defense except a few fascists whose weapon is the bludgeon, we must try once again to look at ourselves in the mirror. We must try to discern our true faces behind the masks, and, despite the distorted features that confront us, to grasp our own truth before the final defacement, which cannot be far off.

I have no intention of doing again what Rutilius Namatianus did long ago or of writing an apology.[1] Nonetheless, when confronted with the mounting hatred and condemnation of the western world and the suicidal frenzy of many Europeans, I, who have attacked the technical society and its scientific rationality, feel obliged to show that there is also a very different side to the West. The West represents values for which there is no substitute. The end of the West today would mean the end of any possible civilization.

vii

I can immediately see the scientists, the sociologists, the historians, and the political scientists wrinkling their noses or their foreheads, depending on the myths they follow. I can hear them saying in accents of scorn: "The West? What is the West? Is there any bond uniting Sweden and Italy? There is no such thing as *the* West: there are a hundred wests! Is there not a greater difference between Spain and Russia than between the Spaniards of the south and the Arabs or between the Russians of the east and the Mongols? Where does your 'western civilization' stop? What are its boundaries? Is it to be found in Europe? But which Europe? Do you include or exclude Russia? Turkey? Is or is not America part of this western civilization?"

The question can, of course, be turned back on the questioner. But I am too familiar with the attempts to compare civilizations not to grasp the weight of the objection. The whole of southern Europe was invaded by the Arabs for centuries on end: the Arabs who brought it everything that made it, from Aristotle to mathematics, from irrigation to mysticism. And the east was invaded and occupied by the Huns, the Hungarians, and so many other peoples. As for Christianity, we must not forget that it came from the east! The West is like St. Mark's in Venice, which was built with the spoils of all the cities, palaces, triumphal arches, columns, and porticos the Venetians had pillaged. There is no distinct thing called the West, but only accumulations of materials derived from all over the place. The West is a set of interactions; and, besides, if our so-called western civilization disappears, it has already spread throughout the world, so that all peoples are now "western"!

Yes, yes, I realize that exact statements on this matter are impossible. I have no intention of getting involved once again in the debate on the possibility of scientifically establishing the data of the social sciences. No one has ever been able to give a precise and satisfying definition of all its concepts, such as class or ideology, and yet without these concepts there would be no such thing as sociology or political science. It is a fact that despite the uncertainty about the scientific character of these sciences men continue to speak about the subjects of them, and they understand one another. We can, therefore, only appeal to "pre-conceptions" and "metalanguage."

In any case, "West" is a word different from all others, and there is no substitute for it. It evokes images and stirs emotions, and these are not false because they *are* the emotion-laden image of the West! The West is a past, a difference, a shared history, and a shared human project, and it is our very life. We may not be able to grasp it clearly or to define it scientifically, but then, in such matters as these, refinement and precision are deadly because they lead to a false sense of intellectual superiority that is won at the cost of a great impoverishment.

In these matters we must be satisfied with rather loose and generic criteria. Sorry to offend you, but being a Frenchman is not the same as being a Chinese. Having a long Christian past is not the same as having a Muslim past. Having conquered the world is not the same as having been conquered. Having created modern science after a millennium of groping is not the same as having repeated the rituals of magic over and over or having accidentally stumbled on discoveries. To have given priority to rationality or the future or "having" is to have set out on a completely different road from that followed by other human groups. That is the sort of thing that serves me as a rough approximation. The West? We know perfectly well what it means!

THE BETRAYAL OF
THE WEST

· CHAPTER I ·

DEFENSE OF THE WEST

1 Guilty, Not Guilty

The West has a bad name these days; in fact, everywhere people are trying to escape from the sinking ship. The West alone is to blame for everything. It has descended on the rest of the world, subjugating peoples who wanted only to live in peace (or so says our new "Story of the Centuries").[1] These peoples were happy, productive, prolific, and well fed; they were ignorant of war, evil, and slavery; they enjoyed security and were supported by philosophy. In other words, the golden age, new style—or not really so new, since the idyllic picture of China or the Arab empire, the Bantu world or the Aztec empire repeats all the noble-minded effusions of the eighteenth century. If there are any proponents left today of the myth of the noble savage, they are surely the people who tell us without a smile of that marvelous world that existed before the Westerner came. All the arts and refinements of life were to be found in that happy world that knew not death or sin or shame, oppression or morality, a world where nature was unhindered and produced the innocent human being.

1

Then along came the West with its train of catastrophes. It came with its mail-clad warriors who were greedy for gold and silver and deceived the poor peoples who received them with the kind of hospitality you might have found in paradise. The soldiers and the traders stole the wealth, enslaved the peoples, and conquered the land. Their very name betrays them: the Conquistadors! They brought terror with them and torture and disease. They set up their illegitimate regimes and reduced the people to utter subjection; they established the colonial system—all to the profit of the parent state. Greed for gold and power was their only motive. They were barbarians far more barbarous than any conquerors before them; some won their way by naked violence, others by virtue; some were boldfaced, others played the hypocrite.

And their missionaries went with them, everywhere destroying healthy natural morals, and imposing an ideology that was nothing but a front for commerce and death. They rooted out the ancient beliefs that were so well suited to the peoples who had developed them. They destroyed cultures and thus the social groupings, leaving the individual isolated where earlier he had fitted so wonderfully into a balanced society. They imposed a morality and introduced these simple souls to evil and sin. They spread abroad the terror of hell and made men feel for the first time the fear of death. These missionaries with their fixation on the cross committed a worse crime than the soldiers and the merchants: they robbed the peoples of their very soul.

Souls were their trade, and the result was total ruin: languages proscribed and replaced by western tongues (German, English, Spanish, French), laws and customs supplanted by those of the invader, who by a single stroke stole honor, dignity, ancestral faith, and the still hidden riches of the earth. Then the invader rewrote history: up to now there had been only darkness and barbarism; he brought civilization. Those who resisted had been nothing but appalling ruffians, Béhanzins,[2] or pirates who did not want these ignorant and underdeveloped peoples to have the happiness and peace that the blessings of science and medicine bring.

Such was the official history taught to schoolchildren, who learned, unconsciously, to think of people with black or red or yellow skins as natural inferiors. Such people were indeed to be pitied by those better off, but they did not deserve the blessings we brought them, because they were rebellious and hypocritical toward us and refused to cooperate with us. Nonetheless (said the official history) many of them, happily, did come to cooperate with us! Many became faithful servants and even defended the fatherland when it was imperiled in 1914. — Lies! Nothing but lies! How can we fail to see that we were nothing but their conquerors, the foreigners who considered them fair game and stole their women and their wealth?

Time has turned on its fragile heel,[3] and we no longer believe the official legends, the nice stories. Our eyes have been opened; we have seen, and are disillusioned. We know the truth now. The truth is that the European came as a murderer, sometimes completely wiping out peoples who wanted their freedom. Thus the countless Indian tribes of North America were first systematically robbed with the help of dishonest treaties and agreements, then ruined in body by the hypocritical gift of firewater, and finally eliminated completely every time they tried to regain their freedom outside the reservations. Why, men used to go off for the weekend to hunt Indians —a far more interesting recreation than hunting partridge!

Latin America experienced the brutalities of men who deliberately spread European diseases so as to cause epidemics and decimate (or worse) the native tribes. We all know the terrible story of objects deliberately contaminated and thrown into the woods so that the Indians might gather them up—and it was the "commissioners in charge of the natives" who did it! In China, Great Britain's persistent policy was to introduce opium into the country and thereby destroy the peoples of Asia. No means was left untried in attaining the single goal of exploiting the wealth of a country and producing goods that would be useful back in Europe. The work force? Slavery, a European invention, supplied that.

The destruction is far from being ended, for the colonial age has now given way to the imperial age. Everybody knows the facts, and we hardly need to mention them. When the world had rebelled against the West and regained its freedom, when the soldiers and the missionaries had departed, the West retained its power and continued its program of exploitation, but by other means. In the process it has become ten times the hypocrite it was before. It controls the economies of the third world and keeps two-thirds of mankind hungry. Thanks to unjust agreements, to the laws of the international market, to a unilateral regulation of prices, and to the use of tariffs, it continues to steal the wealth of peoples who think of themselves as now free but who are in fact financial and economic dependents.

The West keeps the rest of the world locked in a hellish vicious circle. Either these other countries can maintain the industrial structure which, for their own greater profit, the whites installed in place of the ancient cultures based on agriculture (then the countries have commodities they can export, but they die of hunger because they have no foods left for consumption). Or else the countries can try to go back to agriculture and abandon cotton, coffee, cacao, and sugar cane (then they have nothing to export, and they die of hunger because, having nothing to sell on the international market, they can likewise buy nothing there). Multinational corporations enter like cancerous growths into the weak economies of these confused and traumatized nations. All the wealth still flows out to the West, even if now by different ways, and the natives gain nothing from it.

In any case, the nations that were once colonies are now so much under the spell of science and technology that their only dream is to accomplish the feats the white man did before them. The myth of progress—*that* kind of progress—controls their lives. Yet even this economic domination is not enough for the West. The West wants more; it wants even greater control of the strings. And so it undermines the free governments that revolution had given the people, and replaces them with puppet ministers and presidents who will dance to the orders of the great economic powers, with dictators who last only because the western imperialists support them.

Everyone today knows of the empire established by the Central Intelligence Agency (CIA) with its foul deeds and its worldwide plotting. And there is the most recent, but surely not the last, act of aggression by Europe: the advocacy of eugenics, the hypocritical desire to prevent the population growth of the third-world peoples, the alarm at the worldwide population explosion, the famous exponential curve. What conclusion does the West draw? Stop immediately all births in India, Africa, and Latin America!

Such is the picture, and now western man is beginning to realize that it is a true picture. And at least on the left, among the intellectuals, the men of ideals, this new awareness has begotten a strong sense of guilt, a terrible feeling of remorse. Look at what we have done! Look at how we have acted! We look at ourselves in a mirror and we see the dead faces of the starved children of Bangladesh, of the Sahel, of Ethiopia. We open our newspapers and read the accusations leveled at us by the now liberated peoples as they tell us the old story day after day, sharpening our sense of remorse and turning the dagger in the wound. Look at what we have done!

But remorse is not enough. We are filled with rage. We cross the boundary line and take our place beside the poor and the oppressed, in a modern "crossing over to the people,"[4] but one inspired by the same sentiments and producing the same effects. We become iconoclasts toward all that the West represents: everything was bad, everything must be destroyed! Only African art, and even perhaps African science, has been a truly fine thing; only politics as practiced by the Chinese is authentic. The only revolt that is just is the revolt going on in Latin America. We acknowledge all accusations as justified, and we are filled with masochistic rage. Yoga and marijuana, Zen and self-destruction—that's the way to our real liberation! It is the peoples we once oppressed that must free us from the Nessus' shirt[5] we have woven for ourselves. There is no way we can throw off the burden of remorse except to destroy everything that caused it.

Expiation can be made only by destroying the West root and branch, by denying all that is most precious to it: its religion, its morality, its virtues. A purifying anger sweeps over us when we think how our fathers left us a world so corrupt and evil. We are ready to light the pyre and burn the corpse we have discovered in the cupboard of the house we thought so clean. The great day of purgation has come! We must without delay oppose all the imperialist schemes the West has under way!

Awareness has brought a bad conscience with it, and we must get rid of that bad conscience—not only at the individual level by eradicating from within ourselves the whole western legacy, nor only at the cultural level by rejecting the whole European tradition (history, Latin, Greek—all must go), but also by taking concrete steps against CIA imperialism and against that most detestable of all detestable things, South Africa. Of course, the American empire is really the most abominable of all. The trouble is, though, that not everyone is willing to vent his rage on it; people make distinctions. Even as they cultivate their own proud nationalism, the peoples of Europe are not unanimous in condemning the United States. But South Africa! *there's* a splendid scapegoat! It has everything: racism, white exploitation of blacks, the production of such despicable goods as gold and diamonds, dictatorship, moralism, power based on religion, the union of church and state, capitalism in a pure form—everything!

South Africa has one further quality that makes us utterly inflexible: it is a weak state, and we have nothing to fear from it. It produces practically nothing that the industrial economy requires. Its army is doughty when it comes to facing the African nations, but what can it do against Europe? It is not important, either strategically or diplomatically, to any other country. If South Africa disappears, neither the position of the West nor the defense against communism nor the churches will be in any way weakened. So, go to it!

It is in these conditions that the courageous World Council of Churches boldly leads the crusade against South Africa! The Council really can't beat the drum against American racism and American imperialism: all its money comes from the United States. Nor can the Council point the finger at the Soviet Union for persecuting the church or for such minor matters as the invasion of Czechoslovakia: that would only cause more trouble for the good Christians living in communist countries. The Council cannot publicize the various kinds of extortion and other shameful things that go on in all the third-world countries (including those that claim to be leftist): that would only mean the Council was racist. No, it looks as if the World Council cannot say anything to anyone, anywhere, on any subject—except on two that will have no repercussions: Portuguese colonialism and, above all, the abomination of desolation, South Africa. On these two subjects, you can say and do anything without fear of consequences.

At last, Christians and non-Christians, the right and the left, the democrats and the republicans, the little fellows and the important people can all close ranks against the common enemy, the incarnation of unrelieved evil. South Africa is the good conscience the West buys on the cheap.

I ask the reader to try to control his indignation as he reads. I do *not* approve of apartheid or the exploitation of black labor or the production of gold and diamonds. The only point I want to make is that all over the world you can find hundreds of situations and organizations like South Africa, but people carefully avoid denouncing them, because that might prove costly, it might be dangerous. I am saying, then, that the united front against South Africa manifests a widespread cowardice, a *refusal* to see everything else that is going on; it is the expression of a bad conscience latent in Westerners, who are happy for the opportunity to relieve it. With South Africa to pounce on, they are spared the need of an "agonizing reappraisal" with regard to all the other situations.

Against this background I would like now to state my own position. I hope the reader will accept it once and for all, and not forget what I say here as he reads the rest of the book. I admit, then, all the accusations leveled at the West for its colonialism and imperialism; I am the first to come forward for judgment. The French, the English, the Spaniards have committed countless atrocities throughout the world over the centuries: they are all a source of constant remorse for me, an unbearable burden. I do not attempt to disclaim all connection with what past generations have done. I refuse to take the easy way out and point the finger at those shocking ancestors of the fifteenth or the eighteenth century who slaughtered the Aztecs and invented slavery for the blacks. They were *our* ancestors! Their sins yesterday are ours today, because we live today by the profits they gathered yesterday. Our scientific and technological progress is inseparably connected with their conquest of the world.

Anyone who denounces and rejects those ancestors or present-day western imperialism should begin by refusing, for example, to use gasoline or to travel by car or bus or train. And there are countless other things he should stop using. That is why, in my opinion, we cannot clear our consciences cheaply by adopting an anti-imperialist ideology, signing manifestos, and drawing up passionate proclamations. That way, we only share the traditional hypocrisy of the West: we point the finger at the wicked and claim that our own conscience is thereby cleansed. No, the power we possess, our whole way of life, and all the material things that sustain us every day make us connivers, whether we like it or not, with the bloodshed, the looting, the torture, the contempt shown, the slaughters inflicted in the past. We are heirs to all that. We have inherited all the wealth, but we have likewise inherited all the hatred of the conquerors that has accumulated down the years.

We must bear the burden of all those crimes. We have no choice but to regard ourselves as debtors to the rest of the world. We owe back what our ancestors took. When the West gives "aid" to the third world, it is in reality only making restitution (and restoring only a tiny part of what was taken). We can never remove the bloodstains from our hands, because we can never restore life to the people slain and the cultures destroyed; we can never reunite the families torn apart by slavery. As for the tortures inflicted, what payment can we make for such suffering? Nothing the white race has done is alien to me, and I must bear the burden of it. I cannot cultivate a good conscience about it all; I cannot assert my own innocence by claiming that my ancestors were the guilty ones or that the Americans are the guilty ones today.

Am I therefore to become a masochist and reject *everything western*, deny all the values of our world? No! I take a middle ground: I admit the accusations in their full extent, but I do not accept the rejection of the West in its entirety. I accept responsibility for the evil that has been done, but I deny that only evil has been done. I know our civilization is built on bloodshed and robbery, but I also know that *every* civilization is built on bloodshed and robbery. In the face of the pseudo-revolutionary speeches, the sensational news of people joining the guerrillas, the contempt for "white culture," and the inflamed desire to destroy everything that made us great, I reaffirm the value of the West we have known.

I am not addressing these words to the right, because the right is bogged down in a western pride that has nothing to do with what I mean. I am an inflexible "anti-Cartierist."[6] No, what I have to say is part of the examination of conscience the West must undertake; it is necessarily addressed to the intellectuals who have already decided where they stand: anti-imperialist, anticapitalist, antiracist, and thus antiwestern.

It is a shocking thing that the West should have become identified with a fascist movement bent on violence. Such a movement is diametrically opposed to everything the West has wanted and tried to be. Such a movement could never have claimed to represent the West if the other people who seek and transmit the true values of a civilization and are responsible for the renewal of the culture had not too readily scorned and rejected the positive heritage of the western world. Our intellectuals have sunk into a kind of self-destructive rage and lost the meaning of the great western adventure. Then the helmeted athletes thought they could claim the enterprise for themselves once they got rid of the intellectuals.

Once again, I shall not be filing a brief for the West. What I am looking for is a balanced judgment; this is to admit, of course, that what I write presupposes acknowledgment of the West's crimes, and that what I say must be understood against that background. Anyone who believes his hands are clean will learn nothing here.

I am well aware of the final criticism that will be leveled here:

to the extent that you recall the greatness of the West, you put weapons into our enemies' hands and strengthen their position. (This is where the accusation of "objective traitor" comes in.) I have three answers to the criticism. The first is that the criticism repeats the great law of propaganda that Hitler enunciated: "Never admit your enemy is right in even the smallest thing." If you deny that your enemy can say anything true, you are simply a propagandist, and the whole discussion becomes squalid. My second answer is that the best way to overturn the enemy's claims to legitimacy is to make our own the values of the West, to acknowledge the positive legacy of the West, and to seek to be its true heirs. My third and final answer is that if the truth may end by serving the enemy, that's too bad: we must speak the truth, no matter what.

Let me begin by recalling some facts. We have been colonialists and we are now imperialists. Granted. But we did not invent colonialism and imperialism, nor are we the sole actors in these dramas. When the Arabs invaded the whole northern section of black Africa, what was that but colonialism, and indeed something worse than colonialism? And what of the Turkish invasions that created the Ottoman empire? and the Khmer invasions that created the Khmer empire? and the Tonkinese invasion that created the Tonkin empire? and the terrible conquests of Genghis Khan, which were doubtless the most terrible conquests of all, since Genghis Khan probably slaughtered some sixty million people in the course of his reign, or more people than Hitler or even Stalin? and the Bantu invasions that created new invader kingdoms in two-thirds of the black continent? What of the Chinese invasions of a third of Asia? and the Aztec invasions of their neighbors that led to what we are told was the wonderful Aztec kingdom that the fearsome conquerors destroyed, but which was itself in fact nothing but a frightful dictatorship exercised over crushed and conquered peoples? The reason the outside conquest was so easy is that the peoples under the Aztec heel rebelled against their overlords.

All these were exercises in *colonialism*, and brought with them the destruction of cultures and languages, genocide, deportation, the creation of thoroughly absolutist empires. The West showed no originality in this matter. In fact, they were not quite as bad as the other conquerors, nor has their empire lasted any longer than the others! Tell me, what is the greatest colonial power of our time? China, of course, which has occupied such non-Chinese territories as Manchuria, Mongolia, Sinkiang, and Tibet. Next in line comes the Soviet Union with its occupation of Siberia.

But of course we don't attach much importance to that sort of thing, because (we tell ourselves) it is past history now, or because we think of it as a domestic affair of Asiatics or Africans. (We do not, however, consider Hitler's war against the rest of Europe as unimportant, because that took place "between whites." Nor did the Japanese invasion of China leave us indifferent.)

The real explanation, though, is that we don't want to know about those things. But we must look at those facts no less than at the others. Why? Not in order to whitewash ourselves; after all, it is no excuse to say that we have companions when it comes to conquering and invading. The real reason we must have a good grasp of all the instances I have been giving is so that we may learn the truth: we cannot expect to find justice and innocence "somewhere else." The Chinese and the Africans are not free of the sin we acknowledge in ourselves; they have been colonialists no less than we, and they (in the case of the Chinese) are imperialists no less than we. It is not among them that we will find the promised paradise or discover at last the place where a man can become his true self. There is no "other place" where we can wash ourselves clean of the sins the West has committed.

We Westerners have also been great practitioners of slavery. No doubt—but surely we cannot forget that the first to practice it (after the ancient world had disappeared) were the Arabs, the Muslim traders who established slavery in black Africa. When the Westerners came, they simply took over the structures for enslaving black tribes that the Arabs had set up. There is a great deal of romantic talk today about Arab liberalism and Arab humanism, but that is just literary chitchat. Look at the *texts* of Islam, and everything is fine; the same can be said of the Gospel *texts*. But the *practice* of the Arabs in conquest and trade was at least as monstrous as the practice of the Westerners. A final point: the West can be accused of using every possible means of imposing Christianity, but the same accusation can be made against Islam and many other religions. We are not dealing with a trait somehow characteristic of the West.

I have already said frankly that the whole world can accuse the West and that we must accept the accusation and take it with complete seriousness. But please note that we have the right to turn the accusation back on *all* our accusers, and to ask them to show a bit more shame. Let them say their own *mea culpa* and stop trying to stir heaven and earth to riot with shouts of the sins of the West. We are all in the same boat.

I love all civilizations. How could I have chosen to be a professional historian if I didn't? I respect them. I admire them at times for their institutions, cultures, and architecture, and, more profoundly, for the human types they have developed. I have so much love for those civilizations, past and present, that we call traditional societies, that I have frequently been charged with obscurantism, infatuation with the past, and belief in the noble savage.

Almost since the time I reached the age of reason, I have been an utterly severe critic of western civilization as represented by American capitalism and Russian communism. Situated between these two alternatives, Europe had no real existence of its own; at best, it could only choose which of the two was to absorb her. I feel no tenderness toward western civilization, but neither can I share the rage of the intellectuals who furiously trample it underfoot while exalting as models Islamic or Chinese civilization, which they regard as so much superior. I am thinking of the eulogizers of Arabic society who draw their inspiration especially from Maxime Rodinson[7] and tell us without a smile that the battle of Poitiers in 732 was a disaster. Why? Because the Franks, who were coarse, uncultured barbarians, were victorious over the refined, intelligent, civilized Arabian knights; as a result, the world was plunged into savagery, and civilization was set back eight centuries.

We need only walk in the gardens of Andalusia or visit the dreaming cities of Seville, Cordoba, and Grenada, and we will get a glimpse of what France might have become if industrious, philosophical, tolerant Islam had rescued her from the nameless horrors that would later devastate ancient Gaul. Instead, the country was first enslaved by fierce Austrasian bandits, then torn to pieces, covered with blood and tears, emptied of its men by the Crusades, and swollen with corpses by so many wars domestic and foreign. Meanwhile, from the Guadalquivir to the Indus, the Muslim world went from triumph to triumph amid a peace guaranteed by the Ummayad, Abbasid, Seljuk, and Ottoman dynasties.

Claude Farrère wrote these lines in 1912, but they represent quite accurately the thinking of very many French intellectuals. The fear, even the terror, that people felt from the sixth century on in the face of the Arab invasions? Propaganda pure and simple! The Arabic annihilation of the North African peoples, of which only the Berbers and the Kabyles have survived? Invented out of whole cloth! The activity of the Barbary pirates on the Mediterranean (an activity that recent historians have legitimately played down, but not denied)? A mere detail!

The Arabs, then, have always been peace-loving, meek, tolerant, kindly people; it is we dreadful Westerners that have been the evildoers. In self-justification I would like to point out a small matter that has been overlooked: the Arab conquest. For, when all is said and done, it is a fact that the Arabs started out from a limited area and undertook the conquest of immense territories, eastward and westward—territories far more extensive than the Romans ever conquered. But don't you see, the conquest was evidently undertaken solely in the interests of peace! Why, the peoples put on their holiday clothes when they saw the Arabs coming; they were filled with enthusiasm and threw open their cities and their homes!

In response, I can only ask on which side the legend and the propaganda are really to be found! Here we have a pitiless military conquest, the ferocious annihilation of entire populations, and the establishment of strict authoritarian regimes. There is nothing legendary about the repeated massacres of the Armenians, the Greeks, the Serbs, the Thessalians, the Montenegrins, and the Georgians. Wherever the Arabs went, terror reigned. They had poets of the utmost artistic refinement, but these poets delighted to contemplate the impalement of conquered peoples. The Arabs built splendid cities, but they used slaves to build them.

The Arabs undoubtedly had a highly developed civilization, but what price did they pay for it? Our own eighteenth-century society, too, was, highly cultured and refined: that is, part of it was! The situation was the same in the Islamic world. Admittedly, there was economic development in some parts of the Arab empire. Indeed there was, but the development had its dark side as well. No need to wait for the European invasion to have that sort of thing. From the nineteenth century on, the Arab countries were in a state of economic and sometimes political chaos; domestic wars were not a European prerogative, and Islam was torn by them, too.

We need only think here of how the Turkish invaders treated the other Arab peoples wherever they went! Our friend Farrère and his successors seem to forget that the Ottoman empire was built on the ruins of the Seljuk empire, which had gone down in blood under the Turkish sword.

I don't particularly mind the learned articles that contrast Islamic pacifism and tolerance (according to the Koran) with Christian brutality. Note, however, that we are constantly faced with the same intellectual defect: the comparison of one side's principles (the admirable principles of Islam) with the other side's behavior (the shocking behavior of Christians). But that is irresponsible. Principles must be compared with principles (Islam and the gospel) and behavior with behavior (Muslim and Christian). The evidence is, I think, that minorities have been no worse treated in the West than in the Islamic world. The stake at Monségur[8] is no worse that the pyramids of heads cut off by the Abbasid sultans.

The antiwestern frenzy spills over into every area. We are told, for example, that all modern science and thought comes from the Africans. The proof is simple. Our religion comes from the Jews, but where did the Jews get it from? From Egypt. Our science comes from the Greeks, but where did the Greeks get it from? From Egypt. The Egyptians, however, are a black race, real Sudanese. (You need only look at the ancient paintings and the mummies to see that the Egyptians are blacks.) Therefore, the black Africans are the source of all modern thought and science.

Why, then, did the blacks not develop these themselves? Why do we not find this thought and this science on the banks of the Zambezi and the Limpopo? The answer is simple: the white invaders suppressed them! Meanwhile, of course, other Westerners tell us that the Arabs are the source of all western thought. Everyone knows that philosophy can be equated with Averroes, Avicenna, and Alkindi,[9] and that our mathematics in its entirety was the work of Arab mathematicians (we still speak of Arabic numbers!). Plato and Aristotle, Archimedes and Pythagoras are unimportant; they have contributed little in comparison with the real source. African or Arab, it really doesn't matter. Everything is fine, as long as it isn't the Europeans who were the creators.

The other great love of our outraged Westerners is China. China, too, is so much more civilized than Europe, but can hardly claim to have been the source of our civilization. Too bad, for it is perfectly clear that everything backward, shocking, or barbaric in China is the result of western colonization. It was all down in black and white in an issue of *Le Monde* in September 1974. The bound feet of the Chinese women? The refined tortures of the warlords? The bureaucratic rigidity of the mandarins? All imported from the West. And, since women have been mentioned, surely we know the guilt our civilization must bear with regard to women. Recall the obscene twelfth-century discussion, in which it was asked whether women had souls (they even debated the question in a synod), and the response was laughter.

Here I must interrupt. Who said, "Woman is the field in which man sows"? Islam. What civilization treats women with the greatest contempt and brutality? What civilization turns her truly into an object? Islam. As for the debate on the souls of women, listen to this: "You ask whether a woman does not lack soul and intelligence. How can you even ask? Of course, she does! And a creature without soul or intelligence also lacks faith. Woman is destined neither for paradise nor for hell. At her death she simply disintegrates into dust" (Qurban Saïd).[10] And the progressive Colonel Qaddafi said in November 1973 that "physiology demonstrates the eternal inferiority of woman."[11] There you have the authentic, constant teaching of Islam as still maintained by the orthodox. As for the famous question raised by the Christian theologians, there are no grounds for asking it either in the teaching of the Bible or in the teaching of the great theologians and the Fathers of the church; the only reason it was asked in the Middle Ages was the disturbance caused in the West when the Islam teaching began to circulate in France.

Let me repeat: I am not criticizing or rejecting other civilizations and societies; I have deep admiration for the institutions of the Bantu and other peoples (the Chinese among them) and for the inventions and poetry and architecture of the Arabs. I do not claim at all that the West is superior. In fact, I think it absurd to lay claim to superiority of any kind in these matters. What criterion would you apply? What scale of values would you use? I would add that the greatest fault of the West since the seventeenth century has been precisely its belief in its own unqualified superiority in all areas.

The thing, then, that I am protesting against is the silly attitude of western intellectuals in hating their own world and then illogically exalting all other civilizations. Ask yourself this question: If the Chinese have done away with binding the feet of women, and if the Moroccans, Turks, and Algerians have begun to liberate their women, whence did the impulse to these moves come from? From the West, and nowhere else! Who invented the "rights of man"? The same holds for the elimination of exploitation. Where did the move to socialism originate? In Europe, and in Europe alone. The Chinese, like the Algerians, are inspired by western thinking as they move toward socialism. Marx was not Chinese, nor was Robespierre

an Arab. How easily the intellectuals forget this! The whole of
the modern world, for better or for worse, is following a western model; no one imposed it on others, they have adopted it
themselves, and enthusiastically.

I shall not wax lyrical about the greatness and benefactions
of the West. Above all, I shall not offer a defense of the material goods Europe brought to the colonies. We've heard that
kind of defense too often: "We built roads, hospitals, schools,
and dams; we dug the oil wells . . . ." And the reason I shall
say nothing of this invasion by the technological society is that
I think it to be the West's greatest crime, as I have said at
length elsewhere. The worst thing of all is that we exported
our rationalist approach to things, our "science," our conception of the state, our bureaucracy, our nationalist ideology. It
is this, far more surely than anything else, that has destroyed
the other cultures of the world and shunted the history of the
entire world onto a single track.

But is that all we can say of the West? No, the essential,
central, undeniable fact is that the West was the first civilization in history to focus attention on the individual and on
freedom. Nothing can rob us of the praise due us for that. We
have been guilty of denials and betrayals (of these we shall be
saying something more), we have committed crimes, but we
have also caused the whole of mankind to take a gigantic step
forward and to leave its childhood behind.

This is a point we must be quite clear on. If the world is
everywhere rising up and accusing the West, if movements of
liberation are everywhere under way, what accounts for this?
Its sole source is the proclamation of freedom that the West
has broadcast to the world. The West, and the West alone, is
responsible for the movement that has led to the desire for
freedom and to the accusations now turned back upon the
West.

Today men point the finger of outrage at slavery and torture. Where did that kind of indignation originate? What civilization or culture cried out that slavery was unacceptable and
torture scandalous? Not Islam, or Buddhism, or Confucius, or

Zen, or the religions and moral codes of Africa and India! The West alone has defended the inalienable rights of the human person, the dignity of the individual, the man who is alone with everyone against him. But the West did not practice what it preached? The extent of the West's fidelity is indeed debatable: the whole European world has certainly not lived up to its own ideal all the time, but to say that it has never lived up to it would be completely false.

In any case, that is not the point. The point is that the West originated values and goals that spread throughout the world (partly through conquest) and inspired man to demand his freedom, to take his stand in the face of society and affirm his value as an individual. I shall not be presumptuous enough to try to "define" the freedom of the individual. But there is no need that I should: we know well enough, without verbalizing it or defining it, what that freedom means. Look at the way societies have developed. We can legitimately say that all of them have moved from monolithic structures toward more flexible ones in which old bonds are broken; from a stage in which individuals are not distinguished from one another toward true individuation of the members; from an "original community" toward a sum-total of distinct and separated men and women; from a complete absence of freedom and independence toward a progressive assertion of this freedom and an affirmation of the self that brings with it an exigency for liberty and independence.

If you are looking for a line of development common to all societies throughout history, there you have it, and there alone. The development has not, of course, occurred everywhere in the same manner and at the same speed. There have also been retrogressions and reassertions of the group at the expense of the individual; frequently, freedom has no sooner been won than it has been lost or denied or distorted.

When man invented his first tools, he was expressing his will to become free in regard to nature. When he invented language, he was expressing his will to be free in regard to things, a freedom made possible by symbolization and the distance it creates between man and things. When he invented art, magic, and religion, he was expressing his will to become a distinct individual and to differentiate himself progressively from the group of which he was a member. "His will"? We do not, of course, mean a clear, conscious, explicit will; after all, no one can put a name on a state of being for which he is still searching, no one can put a label on it. The "will" in question is a slow, instinctive drive, a blind movement forward that is, however, as strong and vital as the coursing of the blood in the arteries; just as the blood circulates, so this will pushes forward. Man seeks to reach his full stature: he stands upright, he speaks, and he cannot help wanting to be differentiated from others, possessing his own autonomy and accepting neither constraints nor limits. Freedom is always meeting opposition, and the degree of freedom is in proportion to the degree of conquest achieved.

Here is where the contribution of the West comes in. As I have indicated, in this slow, subconscious, spontaneous historical process no one has ever set the goal in advance, no one has *said* what he was seeking, or even expressed what he was about. But it was precisely the meaning of the whole process that the West discovered (not through sociological research, but in the form of a proclamation); the West gave expression to what man—every man—was seeking. The West turned the whole human project into a conscious, deliberate business. It set the goal and called it freedom, or, at a later date, individual freedom. It gave direction to all the forces that were working in obscure ways, and brought to light the value that gave history its meaning. Thereby, man became man.

The West attempted to apply in a conscious, methodical way the implications of freedom. The Jews were the first to make freedom the key to history and to the whole created order. From the very beginning their God was the God who liberates; his great deeds flowed from a will to give freedom to his people and thereby to all mankind. This God himself, moreover, was understood to be sovereignly free (freedom here was often confused with arbitrariness or with omnipotence). This was something radically new, a discovery with explosive possibilities. The God who was utterly free had nothing in common with the gods of eastern and western religions; he was different precisely because of his autonomy.

The next step in the same movement saw the Greeks affirming both intellectual and political liberty. They consciously formulated the rules for a genuinely free kind of thinking, the conditions for human freedom, and the forms a free society could take. Other peoples were already living in cities, but none of them had fought so zealously for the freedom of the city in relation to other cities, and for the freedom of the citizen within the city.

The Romans took the third step by inventing civil and institutional liberty and making political freedom the key to their entire politics. Even the conquests of the Romans were truly an unhypocritical expression of their intention of freeing peoples who were subject to dictatorships and tyrannies the Romans judged degrading. It is in the light of that basic thrust that we must continue to read Roman history. Economic motives undoubtedly also played a role, but a secondary one; to make economic causes the sole norm for interpreting history is in the proper sense superficial and inadequate. You can not write history on the basis of your suspicions! If you do, you only project your own fantasies.

I am well aware, of course, that in each concrete case there was darkness as well as light, that liberty led to wars and conquests, that it rested on a base of slavery. I am not concerned here, however, with the excellence or defects of the concrete forms freedom took; I am simply trying to say (as others have before me) that at the beginning of western history we find the awareness, the explanation, the proclamation of freedom as the meaning and goal of history.

No one has ever set his sights as intensely on freedom as did the Jews and Greeks and Romans, the peoples who represented the entire West and furthered its progress. In so doing, they gave expression to what the whole of mankind was confusedly seeking. In the process we can see a progressive approach to the ever more concrete: from the Jews to the Greeks, and from the Greeks to the Romans there is no growth in consciousness, but there is the ongoing search for more con-

crete answers to the question of how freedom can be brought
from the realm of ideas and incarnated in institutions, behavior, thinking, and so on.

Today the whole world has become the heir of the West, and
we Westerners now have a twofold heritage: we are heirs to the
evil the West has done to the rest of the world, but at the same
time we are heirs to our forefathers' consciousness of freedom
and to the goals of freedom they set for themselves. Others
peoples, too, are heirs to the evil that has been inflicted on
them, but now they have also inherited the consciousness of
and desire for freedom. Everything they do today and everything they seek is an expression of what the western world has
taught them.

The freedom being everywhere sought and being expressed
at all levels has led the peoples along strange ways and produced unexpected consequences. Thus the systematic, effective application of rationality *(technique)* is evidently an effect
of freedom. At the same time, however, it has proved to be the
great force that negates and destroys freedom.

Men have sought freedom in the political realm, and western liberalism achieved it. And yet political, economic, and
juridical liberalism have turned out to be the surest destroyers
of freedom! Marx demonstrated this beyond a doubt. Freedom becomes circumscribed and limited to a small area in
which a man can move freely, like the owner of a garden who
is free to do what he wants there but can't go outside the gate.
The freedom won in the political arena inevitably and in every
case produces the ever more powerful, abstract, and comprehensive state. How strange that the consciousness of freedom
and the will to give it concrete expression should always end
in producing the opposite of what was sought! This conflict
was hitherto specific to the West, but now it has become the
experience of the world at large.

By a similar process conflict and contradiction have entered
the heart of the individual, because freedom has led to constant questioning: nothing is permanently gained, everything
is constantly being called in question by the restless and dis-
satisfied individual. Freedom has produced the bad con-

science, because I, the individual, alone am responsible for what I do, but now I have also become responsible for everything else that happens, and I can not live amid such tension. I never finally achieve anything, but only intend to achieve it, and this very quickly leads to self-accusation. Yet the West, with its sights set on freedom, will continue to proclaim its values and goals and signs, but it will also continue to find itself involved in all that is opposed to freedom.

Not only is the movement of the kind we have been describing; it is also infected with extremism. This extremism is another effect of the consciousness of freedom; in every case, man feels bound to pursue the ideal to the bitter end. Freedom sets no limitations for itself, but commits man to extremes. It is no accident that the theologian of Christian liberty is also the theologian who tells us, "Sin robustly!" *(Pecca fortiter)*. Whatever a man decides to do, freedom commits him to doing it to the full. Any path a man ventures upon, he must follow straight on.

But what qualms of conscience and what self-accusations he experiences as he does so! Why? Because bad conscience is inseparable from freedom. Bad conscience is a turning back upon oneself, a judgment of the self on the self, and such a thing is possible only if one is and claims to be free. There is no freedom without an accompanying critical attitude to the self. Alienation begins when a person becomes monolithic, too much of a piece, a man of a single idea—in short, a maniac. He turns others into objects, but himself becomes an object for others. Then there is alienation indeed, far worse than the kind that occurs in the economic sphere; more exactly, the latter alienation is a concrete expression of the other, far more radical alienation.

The excess of freedom and the critical turning back upon the self that freedom begets are at the source of dialectical thinking and the dialectical interpretation of history; which is to say that they are at the source of history itself. Here again, it is not an accident that the Jews, the people who initiated the idea of freedom, also discovered dialectical thinking in its essentials even before the Greeks came along. This dialectic is more than a philosophical method; it may not be inscribed in the nature of things, it may not be the very movement of history, but it surely expresses what the West experienced as history on the basis of freedom and the whole project of freedom.

Marx was not the founding father in this matter; in fact, nothing began with him. He too was heir to the great movement that has been so specifically characteristic of the West. Nothing in his thinking is explicable or justifiable except as sustained by the movement of freedom and by the unconditional exigencies of freedom. Socialism is simply a relay station in the movement started long ago, for socialism has meaning only in view of freedom just as it has meaning only in view of individuals. When freedom is the goal, there can be no question of fusing men into an undifferentiated collectivity.

It is precisely this contradiction of freedom, however, that is expressed in all the works of the West. The result is extremes of every kind: greatness and shame, utilitarianism and charity, generosity and exploitation, devastation and heightened value, waste and thrift, work and leisure, spoliation and rational methods, expansion and introversion.

The West discovered love, and love is but another face of freedom, although it also brought into play means of gaining power and domination of which men had hitherto been ignorant. The most rational civilization men have yet known also went to extremes in every area. Dionysus and Apollo are inseparable, and each of them expresses that movement of freedom that the West discovered.

Similarly, and as part of the same process, the West brought about the division of societies and the world into rich and poor. Please note, however: I am not saying that there had not been rich and poor earlier and in other parts of the world. The point is, rather, that everything used to be so organized that wealth and poverty were stable states, determined (for example) by the traditional, accepted hierarchy, and that this arrangement was regarded as due to destiny or an unchangeable divine will. The West did two things: it destroyed the hierarchic structures and it did away with the idea of destiny. It thus showed the poor that their state was not something inevitable. This is something Marx is often credited with having done, but only because people are ignorant. It was Christianity that did away with the idea of destiny and fate.

Doubtless there have been Christians who used the notion of "God's will" to determine the order of the world and the distribution of wealth and wretchedness. But that is a deviation from true Christian thought (as Stalin was a deviation from Marx), and in any event it could not suppress the self-assertion of freedom itself. Marx made the Christian line of thought his own and reasserted the authentic message; he is unthinkable without the Christian infrastructure. He is utterly representative of the West in everything he wrote.

Once Christianity had destroyed the idea of destiny or fate, the poor realized that they were poor, and they realized that their condition was not inevitable. Then the social organisms that had made it possible to gloss over this fact were challenged and undermined from within.

Against all this background we can see why the whole idea of revolution is a western idea. Before the development of western thought, and apart from it, no revolution ever took place. Without the individual and freedom and the contradictory extremes to which freedom leads, a society cannot engender a revolution. Nowhere in the world—and I speak as one with a knowledge of history—has there ever been a revolution, not even in China, until the western message penetrated that part of the world. Present-day revolutions, whether in China or among the American Indians, are the direct, immediate, unmistakable fruit of the western genius. The entire world has been pupil to the West that it now rejects.

The Illusion of Freedom, a first-rate film of Luis Buñuel's, offers us a splendid illustration of the perversion of freedom, that freedom which the West discovered and now ridicules. Unfortunately, none of the critics seem to have grasped the real point of the film. Yet the meaning is clear enough, provided we interpret the whole in the light of the opening images.

The starting point for the film is Goya's great picture "The

Execution at Tarragona," with this difference, that the men being shot cry, "Down with freedom!" instead of "Long live freedom!" Moreover, these men are monks, aristocrats, officers—in short, the ancient régime. "What freedom are they speaking of?" some of the critics have asked. Why, clearly the freedom of the French "republican" (i.e., imperial) armies, which, as everyone knows, invaded the rest of Europe in order to bring freedom to all peoples (i.e., to bring the destruction of the old order and the monarchies).

The freedom in question finds expression first in the shooting of opponents and then in the three gestures of the French officer who bolts down some consecrated hosts, kisses the statue of Elvira, and profanes her tomb. Freedom here is the freedom to transgress: no more taboos, no more stupid respect for religion or man, we are free! That is the conqueror's freedom that the men executed at Tarragona are rejecting: a freedom unrestrained by reason or law. Do whatever you want.

The entire film builds upon this opening idea and shows where it leads. The first sketch with its strange dreams evolves out of the primal impulse, which is the horror of symmetry and balance (the actor destroys the symmetry of the mantelpiece by putting an enormous hairy spider on it), and the taste for the incoherent. Next come the reactions of the mother and father to the "obscene" photographs that a depraved old man gives to their little daughter. However, these pictures that the parents judge to be scandalous and pornographic are in fact reproductions of the finest European monuments! They are "obscene" in the etymological sense, but can be regarded as scandalous only if one rejects traditional art and all relationships with the past. In this particular family, these "horrors" are replaced by what is regarded as the height of esthetic taste and beauty: enormous spiders. Here is esthetic freedom, achieved through the rejection of all canons.

Everything becomes relative: we can now gather and defecate together in a worldly manner. After all, eating, too, is a shameful and base occupation, a mere matter of social convention. Eating and defecating, then, are really the same: there's no good reason to treat the one differently from the other.

Freedom, too, in relation to purposes and goals. The doctor finds that the blood analyses and x-rays of his patient are satisfactory and even firstrate simply because they confirm his diagnosis. He pays no attention to the sick person; he has completely forgotten the purpose of his entire activity. Similarly, parents call out the police to look for their daughter who has been living at home. The police do not hesitate for a moment: they exist in order to look for missing persons, and so they rush out on the search, without considering even for a moment the girl who is the object of all this activity. They ask no questions about the purpose of their service, and see no relation between the administrative machine and reality. These policemen follow a course of formation that has been set up by the authorities, yet these same authorities empty the classrooms by sending the men out on a series of calls; the important thing to the authorities is that the course is on the books; they do not care whether anyone really follows it.

Freedom, finally, with regard to the meaning of what one does. Sexual freedom, as when the film shows us the inn and a series of the sexual perversions so lauded by the intellectuals but reduced here to the shabby, grotesque things they really are. The great effectiveness of the film is due to the fact that it is constantly in touch with the real world, that it effortlessly unveils what is grotesque, and that it draws absurd consequences from grandiose principles.

Reality? The man condemned to death is immediately freed and congratulated; people ask for his autograph. Impossible? Not at all! It portrays our society perfectly: a society that has legal codes and condemns the criminal, but at the same time does not dare carry out its sentences; on the contrary, it very shortly exalts and glorifies the criminal. I need only mention the ghastly Jean Genet[12] and that wretched fellow Papillon.[13] There you have our heroes—the heroes of freedom!

The criminal atop the tower fires at random into a crowd. Freedom! He is condemned and congratulated. Freedom! The cops arrest the police chief? So what? Then you have two police chiefs congratulating each other. So what? Everything can be freely done; anything can happen (the dead woman in the burial vault telephones the police commissioner); anything goes (the cops arrest the police chief): it really makes no difference what does happen. At the end the two police chiefs are reunited and go off together to stand freedom up against the wall and shoot her at Vincennes where the university and the zoo have gotten mixed up.

The film is thus a tremendous indictment of the freedom that has become absurd because it has rejected all limits. The absurd and grotesque are the inevitable result of the relativization of all norms and the absence of reason, order, and coherence. Buñuel offers terrifying proof that what the intellectuals exalt as the absurd is indeed absurd and imbecilic in real life; that the incoherence the intellectuals praise in art and poetry is translated into the real incoherence of the idiotic and the comic; that the sexual freedom so much admired is in fact shabby and grotesque. In other words, he shows us the visible reality corresponding to the intoxicating ideas of our avant-garde intellectuals.

The film is a mirror image of Georges Bataille.[14] Over against the freedom that is in fact imbecility the film sets the freedom and grace of the animals, as well as the animals' inability to understand the stupidities in which vaunted human freedom indulges (note the ostrich at the end). The truth is that man possesses freedom only when reason, coherence, and purposefulness reign.

I know I am swimming against the stream. Our conformist Parisian intellectuals place weighty emphasis on the European ethnocentrism that has distorted all perspectives and even all the realities themselves. Europeans, drunk with their successes and conquests, have ignored the splendid civilizations that have flourished outside the West; they have despised other peoples, simply because these peoples had been conquered. The critics, therefore, spend their time calling attention to the value of what is done elsewhere than in Europe.

I have not the least intention of denying these values. Of course, there have been empires and arts, literatures and religions, rational methods and philosophies in other parts of the world! How could anyone deny it? Nor have I any intention of pooh-poohing the value of all these things when found elsewhere or of trying to set up a scale for measuring civilizations and proving that European civilization is the most perfect of all. Who is capable of passing an unconditional judgment on a moral code or a piece of sculpture? No, my concern is simply that we should not reverse the old mistake and end by saying: "Europe, after all, is worth little compared to China."

Today we frequently hear people ringing the changes on the well-known statement that Europe is only a small promontory sticking out from the vast continent of Asia. Well, if civilization is to be measured in square miles, we might also point out that the brain is only a small appendage, weighing fifteen hundred grams at most, to about a hundred and fifty pounds of good food!

Enough of that sort of thing! I wish only to remind the reader that the West has given the world a certain number of values, movements, and orientations that no one else has provided. No one else has done quite what the West has done. I wish also to remind the reader that the whole world is living, and living almost exclusively, by these values, ideas, and stimuli. There is nothing original about the "new" thing that is coming into existence in China or Latin America or Africa: it is all the fruit and direct consequence of what the West has given the world.

In the fifties it was fashionable to say that "the third world is now entering upon the stage of history." The point was not, of course, to deny that Africa or Japan had a history. What the cliché was saying, and rightly saying, was that these peoples were now participating in the creative freedom of history and the dialectic of the historical process. Another way of putting it is that the West had now set the whole world in motion. It had released a tidal wave that would perhaps eventually drown it. There had been great changes in the past and vast migrations of peoples; there had been planless quests for power and the building of gigantic empires that collapsed overnight. The West represented something entirely new because it set the world in movement in every area and at every level; it repre-

sented, that is, a coherent approach to reality. Everything—
ideas, armies, the state, philosophy, rational methods, and
social organization—conspired in the global change the West
had initiated.

It is not for me to judge whether all this was a good thing
or bad. I simply observe that the entire initiative came from the
West, that everything began there. I simply observe that the
peoples of the world had abided in relative ignorance and a
hieratic repose until the encounter with the West set them on
their journey.

Please, then, don't deafen us with talk about the greatness
of Chinese or Japanese civilization. These civilizations existed
indeed, but in a larval or embryonic state; they were approxi-
mations, essays. They always related to only one sector of the
human or social totality and tended to be static and immobile.
Because the West was motivated by the ideal of freedom and
had discovered the individual, it alone launched society in its
entirety on its present course.

Again, don't misunderstand me. I am not saying that European science was superior to Chinese science, nor European
armies to Japanese armies; I am not saying that the Christian
religion was superior to Buddhism or Confucianism; I am not
saying that the French or English political system was superior
to that of the Han dynasty. I am saying only that the West
discovered what no one else had discovered; freedom and the
individual, and that this discovery later set everything else in
motion. Even the most solidly established religions could not
help changing under the influence. We must remember that
the Hinduism which drew such an enthusiastic response from
English spinsters in 1930 and is today inspiring the young with
revolutionary fervor, represents a modernization of the Hindu
tradition through contact with the West. What an incredible
experience the world has undergone due to the West!

It was not economic power or sudden technological advances that made the West what it is. These played a role, no
doubt, but a negligible one in comparison with the great
change—the discovery of freedom and the individual—that
represents the goal and desire implicit in the history of all

civilizations. That is why, in speaking of the West, I unhesitat-
ingly single out freedom from the whole range of values. After
all, we find justice, equality, and peace everywhere. Every civilization that has attained a certain level has claimed to be a
civilization of justice or peace. But which of them has ever
spoken of the individual? Which of them has been reflectively
conscious of freedom as a value?

The decisive role of the West's discovery of freedom and the
individual is beyond question, but the discovery has brought
with it two tragic consequences. First, the very works of the
West now pass judgment on it. For, having proclaimed freedom and the individual, the West played false in dealing with
other peoples. It subjected, conquered, and exploited them,
even while it went on talking about freedom. It made the other
peoples conscious of their enslavement by intensifying that
enslavement and calling it freedom. It destroyed the social
structures of tribes and clans, turned men into isolated atoms,
and shaped them into a worldwide proletariat, and all the time
kept on talking of the great dignity of the individual: his autonomy, his power to decide for himself, his capacity for choice,
his complex and many-sided reality.

The inconsistency between the West's words and actions
only made men take the words more seriously. Because slavery
reigned, the proclamation of freedom ceased to be agreeable
rhetoric and became the fierce demand of the enslaved: freedom or death! Because men had lost the innocence proper to
the group which had been as it were their warm maternal
womb, they were now determined truly to be individuals and
to build their own new society, their republic, their socialist
state. The West's actions were inconsistent with its words; the
result was that the peoples of the earth took the words seriously and turned against the speaker who had shown himself
to be rent within by such a radical contradiction. It is as though
there were a law at work: each man must kill the thing he loves.
The West could not remain benevolently disinterested and be
satisfied to wake the peoples of the world from the sleep of
childhood. No, it had to lead them into a night of horrors so
that they might waken in themselves the desire to emerge into

the light and warm themselves at the fire the West had lit.

The second of the two tragic consequences is this: that if the West is challenged and condemned, there is nothing left! The other peoples are no longer capable of building a new little system for themselves, an autonomous culture, a unique historical experience of their own. Everything depends on the West—and I am not speaking simply of food and machines; I am speaking of the vital dynamic force that drives men. It can be said, then, with full truth, that the West's forfeiture is a dramatic fault that is setting mankind on a new and fateful course. No one today can claim to follow an autonomous path. And yet we see our intellectuals hugging the illusion that China has found "another way."

Is it not perfectly clear, however, that this "other way" is really not other at all and that everything about it—the Marxism, the rational methods, and above all, the very movement itself—is western in its inspiration? It was not "history" or some wonderful initiative of the Chinese sages in discovering their own new way that freed China from feudalism and mandarinism. The Chinese were formed, directed, and driven by the West, and it is western ideas that have given vitality to the whole great undertaking.

(Surely I do not have to repeat that western impulses have not produced a result identical with the West? The driving force—even in China—is the discovery of freedom and the individual. I have never claimed, therefore, that Mao's China is a replica of Pericles' Greece or Victorian England. If it were, we would have to say that the Chinese were really not inspired by the West's discovery after all.)

All the peoples of the world are now living on the western heritage and on the impetus received from the West. If either is challenged or denied, if the West is rejected, all the peoples of the world will forfeit their very possibility of existing in the future. You can reject the European nations, you cannot reject their civilization. The world has become western in becoming one. To attack the West is to attack the entire world (as I have shown in another book, *Autopsy of Revolution,* [15] the revolution the world needs can still take place effectively only in the

West). Are we to be swollen with satisfied pride that such power is ours (a power far greater than that of the CIA or the multinational corporations)? By no means. The situation of the West brings with it, on the contrary, a crushing responsibility—and perhaps a crushing guilt.

The guilt I mean is not simply guilt for having destroyed the other cultures (this was the result chiefly of the application of rational methods). It is guilt chiefly for having set mankind on a road that we know from experience leads nowhere; for having driven men to seek a freedom they cannot effectively realize in their lives; for having stirred men to fierce demands and having awakened hopes that have been disappointed in our own case. It would have been better to let mankind go on sleeping. And yet such is the path on which men's feet are now set; any other existence would doubtless seem drab, mean, and insipid. Freedom may perhaps turn the world into a chaotic hell, but once the possibility of freedom is glimpsed, nothing else can satisfy man.

What we have said of freedom can be said analogously of history. It would be stupid, of course, to think that the African peoples or the American Indians "had no history," as though having a history were a western privilege! It is perfectly clear that every part of the world has had its history and that its history began with the origin of man. It is nonetheless true that the West "discovered" the fact and became aware that man has and is a history. Nowhere else—not in Islam (despite the chroniclers) or in China (despite the archives of the mandarins) or in India—did anyone discover the astounding truth that is peculiar to man: he is a maker of history, history understood as the expression of freedom and of man's mastery of events, nature, and his own social life.

This conception of history is characteristic of all western thinking, whether rightist or leftist. Reflect and you will realize how close to each other, despite apparent opposition, are the conception of man as maker of his history (Marx) and the now outmoded historiography that concentrated on "great men" (these latter, after all, being but the models, archetypes, and most visible incarnations of something the Marxist sees real-

ized in every man). Whether you study Napoleon or the proletariat and claim that the one *or* the other is the maker of
history, you are pursuing the same basic line of western
thought, namely, that man is, has, and makes history.

If Africa and Asia are now discovering their own histories,
it is because they are accepting the vision of man and time that
the West has brought to them. This is so despite the fact that
the West, caught up in the same old contradiction, denied
them their history and wanted to keep history as its own prerogative; the explosive force of the idea shook the world despite the West's efforts.

Now, after discovering history and thereby stimulating
human self-consciousness to an extraordinary degree, the
West is betraying itself. The science of history is being
drowned by an accumulation of proofs, mathematical analysis,
and the most insipid kind of rationalism.[16] Testimony is
becoming a negligible quantity, and historical criticism is turning psychotic and obsessive. All this began among the scholars
dealing with the origins of Christianity. At that point textual
exegesis turned into a kind of madness, the more so in that the
stakes were so high. The non-Christians took the rational approach to history and used "method" to prove that everything
in the texts was false. The Christian historians, anxious not to
seem influenced or even deformed by their "religious" convictions, adopted the same approaches and methods.

The result was that a pseudo-science of history, a criticism
that was not scientific at all but merely partisan, undermined
everything. The structure thereby dismantled was one of the
very foundations of the West; the West set out to destroy it
because of the rage bad conscience had produced and because
it thirsted for a justification other men would accept, while
it rejected the justification that comes to all men from God.
At the same time, the West was destroying its own science
and making it ridiculous. An example will show how greatly
the shadow of suspicion can darken history: *Le Monde,* in its
issue of August 10, 1974, published a mind-boggling letter
from a professor of humanities that casts doubt on Hitler's
gas chambers:

Were the gas chambers myth or reality?. . . Has your opinion on whether they were real varied since 1945? . . . I have thus far seen no photographs that seem certainly authentic. Neither the Center for Jewish Documentation nor the Institute of Contemporary History at Munich have been able to provide me with such probative pictures. Do you know of any?

Let us not think the professor is an isolated instance. He expresses the same intellectual attitude as the historians who for two centuries have been rejecting the testimonies to the resurrection of Christ. They, too, would have needed a photograph to convince them. History is becoming idiotic—in both senses of the word! After all, how can a photograph be probative? If someone came up with perfectly authentic photographs of gas chambers, would they have really convinced the professor? No, not even if the photos showed lines of condemned people entering the chambers. Even if we had photos of the interior of gas chambers with men dying there, would we really be sure, after all, that this was the Nazis' work? And so on, and so on. There is no such thing as absolute proof. Our historical science, by its mad search for such proof, has progressively rendered meaningless the history that the western genius discovered.

2   Defense of Western Man

It is a remarkable and easily verifiable fact that, while western man has claimed to be an individual, he has never embodied and expressed freedom in his manner of life.

Western man has been a conqueror, motivated by the thirst for power, and in this respect he is like all the other conquerors of history. That kind of action is not specific to him; on the contrary, it makes him indistinguishable from many others. There is, however, another kind of "conquest," and the thing I regard as singular and indeed unique about western man is the universal mastery he has sought in every area: mastery of things through reason and the application of rational method, mastery of human relations, mastery of himself. The emphasis here is on "universal," for other peoples have gained mastery or control in one or other area (think of the well-known self-control of the Chinese and the impassivity of the Japanese) and have gone much further in it than Westerners. Western man, however, is the only one, it seems to me, who has sought for mastery of everything without exception.

The mastery or control is nonetheless an ambiguous thing. When it has been applied to the world and to things, it has proved to be in the last analysis nothing but greed and harsh possessiveness. When it has been applied to other individuals, it has proved to be a desire for power and domination. But the quest for control has been undertaken no less intensively in man's inner life than it has in the outer world where it catches our attention, and in the inner world, too, the control has proved to be ambivalent. No human group has ever implemented so fully the will to rationalize everything and to dominate the world of ideas no less than the world of things.

This is the other side of the discovery of freedom and the emergence of the individual. The free individual inevitably became a force moving outward to dominate the world and others, but the same individual was also, and inseparably, bounded and imprisoned by his methods and the mastery he had achieved. He could do nothing save in a totally coherent way. He made the appalling discovery that he had created for himself an inner limitation, namely, the necessity of applying rational method to everything he undertook and everything he claimed.

At the interpersonal level, the individuals who had discovered themselves and distinguished themselves each from the other, and who were gifted with the capacity for embarking on new and original undertakings, could enter into relations with one another only through the mediation of a code that was manmade and prevented direct and therefore brutal or even savage contact (a juridical code or a code of manners), or through rituals that were not external but internal and required complete self-control.

Three remarks are called for here. The first can be put as a question: In my description of western man am I harking back to the eighteenth-century idea of man as an individual and necessarily endowed with reason? Am I making reason the specific characteristic of man? By no means. Reason is not something given, a necessary product of the brain, somewhat as we necessarily have arms and legs. The mistake of the eighteenth-century philosophers was to believe that what had gradually come into being in the western world, what had slowly and with difficulty been brought to birth over the centuries since the days of Greece and Rome was a self-evident product of nature. Their error was to think that reason was given with human nature. In fact, it was the very idea of "nature" that caused them to make this mistake, as we can see from other foolish statements of theirs, such as that man is free by nature or that "men" are born free and equal.

Not so! Freedom was something unexpected and incomprehensible, attained through a long slow process. That is why it is so odd to see Rousseau claiming, on the one hand, that man is endowed with reason, and on the other, attacking in a most violent fashion the laws, customs, and courtesies men follow. He did not realize that laws, customs, and good manners represented a set of processes necessary for man if he was to control his own action, processes that were all the more necessary in the degree that he became free and fully an individual.

In my view, then—and this is my second remark—we are not dealing with a reason that is natural, nor is the man of the western world a product of nature. He is not an expression of a "human nature," but is, in the fullest sense of the terms, something invented, something artificial, something slowly created in the course of history. Western man is not "man as such" or "man in himself." He is only one of many possibilities, for he is the result of a special historical process and the product of certain choices (repeated, cumulative, assembled into a whole, but also, in part, unconscious).

We, too, are now confronted with a choice: Shall we continue to will western man? We must make this choice with the clear understanding that if we cease to make it, western man will cease to exist. We cannot go on indefinitely flouting reason and freedom. We Westerners at the present time are treating our world and the human type it has produced in exactly the same way as the technicians (the masters of rational methods) have, in the view of the ecologists, treated the air, water, oceans, and forests. The technicians thought these things were so vast and inexhaustible that they could do anything they wanted with them: "Pour millions of tons of waste into the ocean—the ocean will always be there." Not so! We are suddenly discovering that the ocean is dying—and we are panicking.

People sit lightly to the countless attacks being made on western man by philosophers, linguistic scientists, structuralists, Marxists, etc., because in their hearts they are so deeply convinced that the individual and reason are utterly imperishable. Surely, then, they can allow themselves the pleasant luxury of questioning and even denying the individual and reason and of exalting the value of madness and the utterly irrational. Artaud then becomes the model, saint, and hero, the master of men's thinking and the new embodiment of the absolute; of course, all the pretty talk about Artaud takes a quite rational form.[17] Lacan may stutter because of genius, the way the Pythian oracle did on her tripod, but he retains the most rational form of social behavior in regard to money.[18] So, too, the great haters of the individual and of western society—the Sollers[19] and the Foucaults[20]—pursue a literary and academic career that follows a very rational plan and is completely western in type.

People are sure, then, that what they attack is so solid and deeply rooted that they can with impunity take pleasure in striking out at it; the whole business is, after all, just playacting and gives them a chance to be the hero. Unfortunately, it is not that at all. Western man is a deliberate and fragile construction. He came only slowly to his full form, and burst into consciousness only in the eighteenth century. Western man existed, of course, before the eighteenth century, for he came upon the scene gradually over the ages, his course marked by successes and failures, splendid advances and retreats. Auerbach in his extraordinary book *Mimesis* has given us a sketch of how western man's grasp of reality developed and how at the same time a certain type of human being was being shaped and formed.[21]

This new type was the product of slow but energetic development, intense self-study, a concentration of all the human powers upon a single point, an accumulation of carefully ordered strata, and a treasure jealously preserved, passed on from generation to generation, and enriched at each successive stage of transmission. Reason did not suddenly come into existence or spring fully armed from the head of Jove, but developed in the process of a bitter struggle with things, the world, society, and the self. It has become the most polymorphous and effective of tools, and, at the same time, a discipline that shapes the personality. It has become the key that seems able to open all locks, and, at the same time, a form of mastery that requires many sacrifices for its acceptance. It is something deliberately chosen, not a gift.

The eighteenth century looked upon the power and omnipresence of reason as so self-evident that it ignored the slow development, the production of reason through a historical process, and proclaimed it to be something universal and the measure of all things. In any case, it is no accident that the eighteenth century was such a brilliant period. Its music was an expression of reason, but that did not prevent its also being an expression of the most lively sensibility in Mozart; the same must be said of painting and Watteau. Reason is not to be compared to a fleshless geometric figure. It is an instrument of incredible range that, even before men became reflexively aware of it, made possible the poetry of Racine, the writing of the *Pensées,* the music of Bach, and the painting of Latour. Nor was it an accident that the century which became fully aware of reason also developed the most refined code of manners— no surprise, because the same impulse was at work: reason is not the same as the rational or rationalism.

It goes without saying that reason makes room for esthetic and relational processes, because reason is a certain attitude toward the world and men; thus, when human relations become difficult, reason produces reasonable behavior and good manners. In every instance where reason is at work, it establishes a hidden procedure which implies, as we said earlier, a mastery or control, whether of the self or of relationships or of thought.

It must further be observed that reason, like law or manners, does not produce a mutation of the entire being. A man does not become radically reasonable or rational. No, the nine-tenths of the iceberg is still under the surface: the drives and the muttering passions, the bottomless subconscious, the unconscious; the waves of lava that shoot up from the bottom of the volcano; the beast that is coiled to leap; the archetypes and the profound images that people man's dreams. Up on top, at the surface, there is the mastery, the control: the effort to sublimate and channel the savage depths, the torrential passions; the effort to develop correctly thoughts that if left to themselves would spontaneously express themselves in inarticulate cries, exclamations, prayers, and curses; the effort to censor words and actions that of themselves would express our animality or our dreams.

The sleep of reason begets monsters. How right Goya was! He saw reality as it really is. Control is but an ever-threatened achievement, a thin film, a layer of oil that calms the waves of the raging sea or, rather, prevents them from breaking and thus allows the boat to stay afloat when logically it should have sunk. You may think, then, that in play or out of vanity or for the sake of notoriety you are attacking a rock so solid that it may crack but will not fall apart; in fact, however, you run the risk of destroying the fruit of man's finest and most perfect self-conquest. How much more prudent Freud and Marx were! How much more respectful they were of reason and the victory and discipline it represents, than you, its faithless heirs, are! Your attacks are destroying and pulling to pieces the loftiest and most fragile of man's conquests. The conquest was embodied, fleetingly and surely in a very imperfect way, in western man, but only as in a model that could be made more perfect.

I have already said that the discovery of reason and self-mastery did not apply to the whole of the human being; it did not express the spontaneous levels of man or suppress everything else in him. I must add now—and this is my third remark —that the model was not adopted by all men of the western world at all periods. There were regressions and withdrawals.

But that is simply to say that reason is like freedom in that it is not like a universally possessed and constantly growing hoard; it is, rather, an enterprise that is constantly under threat and must walk the narrow line between sclerotic repetition and spontaneous explosion.

Not all western men, then, can be taken as examples of the discovery of reason, of the embodied act of reflexive self-awareness. But in all of them there was an unconscious thrust toward this model and an obscure sense of condemnation when the goal was not attained. In all there was a vague but profound acceptance of the intuition and of the intention of someday producing a human being who would at last be both reasonable and free.

There is, then, a choice to be made, but it must be made openly and deliberately. The typical vice of our age is the underhand, undeclared attack. People are seemingly bent on preserving all the accomplishments of the western world, but in fact they are attacking the planned construction and scattering its components to the winds of passion and of a series of inconsistent commitments. No, you must choose. Here again, you cannot have everything and pile up every possible advantage.

Does being a man mean surrendering to the drives of the unconscious, the wild surges of irrationality, the conditioning imposed by physiology, the explosive bursts of desire, and the onrush of hatred? Am I a man when I couple like the beasts, driven by the desire for momentary pleasure and with no thought of the morrow? when I let myself go in wild rage? when I plunge into the unconsciousness produced by drugs and liquor? Does Silenus (who, let us not forget, is inseparable from Dionysus) reveal man's true face to us? We are too ready to do honor to Dionysus: the beautiful, the unrestrained, the free, the god of dance and feast and wine. We see only that side of him, but in fact he is also Bacchus, hideous and ridiculous; he is Silenus, the repugnant potbelly. How easy to forget about Silenus and keep only a glorified image of the god! How easy to forget the frightful dehumanization and irreversible debasement of the drug addict, his complete alienation, his deadly dependence on a chemical to preserve the illusion of a freedom to soar and go on journeys, the marvelous hallucinations, the dreams, the supposed transcending of the human condition. That is a point we must come back to.

Is *that* what it means to be a human being? The West's answer has been an unconditional No. But we should remember that the West was not alone in giving that answer; it was the answer given by humankind from the beginning. If the animal who gradually named himself man even as he had given names to the other animals had been satisfied to obey his instincts and give immediate expression to his drives, if he had not repressed, ritualized, and symbolized, if he had not created the disciplined life and social organization that have restraint for their foundation, he would simply have disappeared. He was, after all, the least capable and the least adapted of all the animals.

For this reason I regard as utterly simplistic the theories that make man a product of chance and necessity. It is agreed that the brain was the specific agent of hominization; it is also agreed that the brain is a complicated collection of billions of electrical connections and impulses. But there must have been more to it than that. This brain had to be used (and this use is not something self-evident). It was destined not only to produce analyses of situations and concrete, technical discoveries, but also to serve the goal of self-mastery and the internal repression of spontaneous animality that self-mastery required. The brain was destined to make possible the apprehension of a connection between self-repression and self-preservation!

None of all that was pre-given. So you really explain nothing by appealing to the "miracle of the brain," any more than you do by using statements such as "man is a social animal."

Man managed to live a human life only in the measure that he *organized* himself into a *society.* (Some profound thinkers claim, of course, that this development was a disaster and that it would have been far better if man had not survived. The animal and plant worlds did not need this troublemaker, but were fine by themselves. On the other hand, these thinkers can think these thoughts only because man has in fact survived! Well, at least they do us a service by making it clear just what the aim is of all the countless movements that worship spontaneity, instinct, and the irrational, and launch violent attacks on western man.) I deliberately use the word "organized," for the wandering horde, the shapeless mass of "human" beings, never existed.

As a matter of fact, we are becoming increasingly aware that even the orangutan pack and the elephant herd are organized, and this in a hierarchical way that brooks no opposition. Man has largely moved beyond this stage; what turned him into man was his *choosing* to organize with the help of mediations (religious, verbal, esthetic, social). The human horde never existed because the human group itself is mediator of a code for each of its members. There is nothing human about "joyous" spontaneous animality or the direct expression of needs and passions. For man, everything is mediated, reflective, deferred. Man does not exist apart from a group, and the group does not exist without exercising a repressive activity.

Civilization has always advanced through successive acts of repression, and to these man has responded, not by an absurd unleashing of the young hound that falls into a frenzy because it is tied up, but by sublimation. The drives that were curbed were directed toward a deeper, more important, more essential object. Thus bridled sexuality stimulated the discovery of new mediations, and each mediation led to an improvement of the group and the individual, an advance in humanness and away from animality. The human being created himself only through successive acts of repression, which, however, were *on each occasion simultaneously rejected and transcended.* Sublimation is not a kind of vague self-consolation: "I would like to do this, but they prevent me, so I'll withdraw into dreams." That is simply foolish. Sublimation means that energy restrained and held within bounds finds a narrow outlet and expresses itself far more powerfully. The stronger the resistance, the more intense the heat produced. The narrower the riverbed, the stronger the current.

People often overlook the fact that the unemotional balance of Apollo hides an array of muscle far more formidable that anything underlying the incoherent gesticulations of Dionysus. Sublimation is what has made man and his world, and is not to be thought of as something he had to fall back on for lack of anything better. But when we speak of "repression" in this context, what do we mean? Initially, there was the purely external repression exercised by the group; specifically, the pressure from the leader (grounded in his physical power) and from the eldest and the elders, which gave expression to a pressure being exercised by the whole context and sustained by the weight of the group as brought to bear on the nonconformist. This kind of pressure had an integrating effect, so much so (as we noted earlier) that there was almost no distinction between the individual and the group.

A further step was taken with the achievement of individuality and freedom. Yet even this was not enough; there was also need of repression exercised from within. The rules of behavior (everything that later was transmuted into law, morality, etc.), the rules for relations between individuals, and organizational structures all became so profoundly a part of the human being that visible, concrete repression was rarely needed. What we have here is the phenomenon of acculturation, that is, the interiorizing of the norms of the group, then of the society at large. The process goes so far that the norms come to seem a direct and personal expression of the individual himself. They seem to emerge from his nature, to be part of his conscience, and to constitute the primordial, inviolable part of the self, whereas in fact they are the effect of the group as it lays hold of the inner depths of each member.

The movement toward freedom leads the individual to call in question first of all (but constantly) the external constraints imposed by the group, which exists independently over against the individual, and of the power installed in the group; but it also leads the individual to challenge the conditioning produced within him by acceptance of social taboos, and to reject the norms he has interiorized. The movement toward freedom thus creates a striking new situation, which cannot be expressed by saying that the individual reverts to an animal state.

According to Konrad Lorenz's theory of aggressivity (which certainly makes some interesting points), it can be said that men have progressively created constraints for themselves in order to put bounds to their aggressivity; it must also be said, however, that the constraints are not always the same constraints and, second, that the will to be free is constantly challenging these restraints.[22] Since, however, all social life would become impossible and even unthinkable in such conditions (as we can see by looking, for example, at how freedom has worked in the economic area), another type of control made its appearance. This was the miraculous discovery made by the West. The West proposed another set of restraints: reason and then all the means that can be grouped together under the rubric of "self-control."

If the individual rejects every external restraint imposed by society, then he must be capable of restraining himself; in other words, he must possess tools that will enable him to make "good use" of his freedom or will prevent freedom from degenerating into the inconsistent behavior of the savage. Reason makes it possible for the individual to master impulse, to choose the ways in which he will exercise his freedom, to calculate the chances for success and the manner in which a particular action will impinge upon the group, to understand human relations, and to communicate. Communication is the highest expression of freedom, but it has little meaning unless there is a content which, in the last analysis, is supplied by reason.

Reason is thus a structure deliberately built to balance the possibilities inherent in the freedom that has been won. Reason does not represent a "trick" but is really the result of an effort to find something that is neither an external constraint nor interiorized social imperatives and that will allow a man to be free and yet at the same time choose a behavior and express opinions which are communicable and can be recognized as acceptable and shared by the other members of the tribe. Here precisely we have the magnificent discovery made by the West:

that the individual's whole life can be, and even is, the subtle, infinitely delicate interplay of reason and freedom.

This interplay achieved its highest form in both the Renaissance and classical literature since the Enlightenment. No other culture made this discovery. We of the West have the most rounded and self-conscious type of man. For, the development of reason necessarily implied reason's critique of its own being and action as well as a critique of both liberty and reason, through a return of reason upon itself and a continuous reflection which gave rise to new possibilities for the use of freedom as controlled by new developments of reason.

The development of reason and freedom was matched by the development of "self-control." A human being cannot be truly free unless he controls himself sufficiently to be found acceptable by others. This implies a mastery of impulses, desires, and spontaneity, not in order to extinguish these but in order to channel them so that they do not seek their expression in unreflecting resentment, anger, envy, and sexual activity. Self-control is, of course, something man learns, and is therefore a form of interiorized social behavior. Such behavior is not reason, but at the same time it is radically different from obedience to taboos. In self-control, the individual is called on simply to master the impulses that lead to animal behavior, and to do so in order to make social relations possible for himself.

Self-control can undoubtedly lead to stupid behavior when the person simply accepts unfounded, involuntary stereotypes. That kind of self-control has often enough been criticized and ridiculed in regard to the English of the nineteenth century. However, the self-control that enables the individuals to *choose* between passions and forms of behavior is a sign of freedom, whether you like to think so or not. The person who is shaken by violent anger and gives vent to it in cries, gestures, insults, and blows; who the more he externalizes it, the more he is carried away by it ("carried away": how expressive!); and who ends up in a paroxysm of murderous rage—such a person is not free at all. We see freedom effectively at work in the man who strictly controls his anger and sets bounds to it, forces himself to be calm, does not raise his voice when everything is boiling up inside him, makes no gesture that is not deliberate and measured even though his heart is pumping, and expresses his anger only in carefully chosen words; the man who later on will not express an opinion about the person who provoked the anger.

I have admittedly taken a very simple example, for control of the passions is not the only condition for freedom. There must also be control of language, ideas, and social relations. Without such control, freedom becomes simply a kind of overflow, with the personality dissipating itself as it seeks unreserved expression.

One expression of self-control is good breeding.[23] It is this that enables men to live together while avoiding the many occasions for conflict and broken relationships. There is no *single* code of manners or good breeding; in fact, there is no single fixed *content*. Every group and every period of western history has drawn up a different code. The important thing is that there be good manners to lubricate the social wheels so that they will not jam. Precisely to the extent that a group is made up of individuals bent on autonomy and freedom, this thin protective film is required so that severe clashes may be avoided. Or, to change the image, there must be this narrow strip of neutral ground separating each individual from his fellows; it provides ground on which men can meet without conflict, simply because the rituals and customs are unimportant in themselves and can be learned by all, giving them a common gathering place but in no way impinging on or compromising freedom and reason.

The whole business becomes absurd, of course, when people regard the rituals as valuable in themselves, when good breeding ceases to be a protective film of oil or a common ground for meeting and becomes instead a straitjacket, when so high a price is set on it that it turns into an inviolable institution. Then good breeding prevents any basic or personal matters from ever being discussed, and so it really prevents one individual from encountering another. When things reach this stage, the code must certainly be jettisoned, but men must, in ridding themselves of it, be conscious of the price they pay and the risks they run.

I am quite aware that many peoples outside the West have also elaborated codes of manners, especially the peoples of Asia, but in these cases the code has a quite different meaning and occurs in an entirely different context. Western good breeding gradually emerged beginning in the fifteenth century (just as it had emerged, under similar circumstances, in Athens and Rome long ago) as individuality developed and the urge to freedom became more concrete. It thus represents an entirely new phenomenon.

Reason combined with control leads to coherence. When the individual wins his freedom from the social body and wants to be free in the face of (i.e., among and against) others, he runs the great risk of incoherence. We have seen how real this danger is from many of the prophets who proclaim spontaneity, the reign of man's deep-rooted energies, and immediacy. "Today," they tell us, "I can be the exact opposite of what I was yesterday." The coherent or cohesive personality is essentially a product of the West.

Here again we must insist that coherence is not the same as repetition or ritualization; it does not mean an unbroken pattern of socially guided behavior. Coherence is connected, on the one hand, with the discourse of reason and, on the other, with the possibility of sustaining an ongoing relationship with others. If a relationship is to be authentic, the other must be able to rely on the continuity of my behavior, for instance, and know that he can expect certain kinds of words of help or refusals from me. Without such continuity a relationship becomes impossible. The continuity provides a guaranty comparable to that afforded by the ritualization of relations; the difference is that the continuity arises *after* individuation and the assertion of freedom, not before.

How important such coherence is may be seen from the judgments men pass on incoherence, and the catchwords they use to describe it: the turncoat politician, the intellectual who changes his ideas like his shirt, the man who becomes infatuated with every woman and deserts them one after another, the fellow who lets his pals down. The judgments embodied in these familiar phrases show that people expect others to maintain a certain continuity or coherence in their behavior. You can't fool others all the time. When confronted with this kind of variability, people infer a basic instability of personality.

To be free, then, means acknowledging what others expect of one (and if one refuses to meet their expectations, it must be for good reasons). It means being capable of accepting the consequences of one's words and actions and behavior, and taking responsibility for what one has done and been. To be untrue to oneself because one refuses to accept this kind of responsibility is not a way of being free; it simply manifests a personality that is without shape or structure. On the other hand, the coherence that may find expression in self-restraint shows that I, for example, have indeed achieved freedom from my own impulses. And if I refuse to honor a commitment, it must not be because I have suddenly got a new idea or am moved by passion; I must know clearly what I am doing and why I am doing it.

Coherence enables me to regard my commitments to others as durable. Marriage or a contract are not mere external formalities; they are meant to be declarations of intentions that are firm and fully accepted. Only then will I succeed in not becoming the inconstant prey of circumstances. Inconstancy in relations between the sexes is surely not an advance in freedom, but a withdrawal from true personhood, for it indicates the inability to resist circumstances and the impulse of the moment. Just think of the countless novels since *Madame Bovary* that have justified adultery and a way of life contrary to "bourgeois marriage." What do we find in them? Everything is the outcome of *circumstances:* a delightful evening, a ball, etc., etc., throw people into one another's arms, people who want the marvelous experience of "free" love, unhindered by the conventions of the kind of marriage society will accept. But such free love is in fact no better than the marriage it rejects, and in addition it inevitably leads to incoherence in sexual relations. Many today think this incoherence marks the end of the end; perhaps it is at least a sign of the coming end.

Let me return to my main argument. It was the West that established the splendid interplay of freedom, reason, self-control, and coherent behavior. It thus produced a type of human being that is unique in history: true western man. (I repeat: the type belongs neither to nature nor to the animal world; it is a deliberate construct achieved through effort.) I am bound to say that I regard this type as superior to anything I have seen or known elsewhere. A value judgment, a personal and subjective preference? Of course. But I am not ready on that account to turn my back on the construction and on the victory and affirmation it represents. Why? Because the issue is freedom itself, and because I see no other satisfactory model that can replace what the West has produced.

In the course of this slow ascent of reason, the West enabled the world to make an almost unbelievable step forward by linking rationality to language. For we must not forget that linguistic science deals first and foremost with languages that are directly or indirectly the product of western reason. Rigorously intelligible and strictly patterned language is a creation of the West. We have perhaps sacrificed a good deal in the process: nuances, classification, myth, magic, creativity, and evocative power, but in return language has become the precise instrument of precise thinking. It has become the apparatus for this kind of thinking, and now possesses its own correctness and uniqueness (and is subject to the dangers its good qualities bring with them). And, let us not forget, it has made possible a remarkable growth of consciousness, the emergence of the individual, and the supremacy of intelligence.

Here again, while acknowledging the price we have had to pay and the losses we have suffered, I am not ready to turn my back on this marvelous embodiment of reason in language, this sovereign instrument, and on the meaning that is bound up with this linguistic structure: meaning that has been transmitted and is now a common possession.

The West is the world of the word that incarnates reason,

of logical, reasoned discourse, Man invented the word; civilizations invented discourse. Many kinds of discourse were possible: the West abandoned mythical discourse, the magical formula, the identification of word with action, the esotericism of prophecy and poetry, the condensation of reality into ritual, and the exaltation of incantation; instead, it followed a new path and developed reasonable discourse.

Yes, yes, I know: "Reasonable discourse weakened and impoverished the word." But I am not claiming that in the marvelous concert of discourses which the various cultures have developed, any one of them is superior, or any one of them useless. Besides, reasonable discourse may indeed be impoverished in the meaning it conveys, but has it not enriched, augmented, strengthened, and completed the word spoken in many, many other kinds of discourse? Humankind would still be in its childhood stage if the West had not taught it continuous, reasoned discourse. The adult undoubtedly loses the powers of the child. You cannot have everything; you cannot simply accumulate. There is no such thing as progress pure and simple; each step forward, each new experience, each innovation requires a letting go of something, even a desertion.

Reasonable discourse was the mark of the West from the beginning. It manifested a mastery of oral expression and a control of the thought processes, which in turn presupposed a control of sensations and feelings and a tenaciousness in face of the self and the milieu. In addition, reasoned discourse supposed the coincidence of thought and its formulation, the adequation of the real as experienced and the real as expressed, and an exact correlation between the word spoken and the word understood. In short, both speaker and hearer had to be master each of his own thoughts and words and feelings.

Reasoned discourse presupposed, finally, that the real itself was marked by continuity. The real ceased to be made up of fragmentary experiences that lacked cohesion with one another and were incommensurable. Time, too, has to be continuous and, in the final analysis, linear as well, since reasonable discourse advanced through a succession of continuous propositions. Before and after were no longer subjective judgments, since in the reasoning process and the continuous discourse there was a linking of clear terms which irrevocably conditioned each other.

All these affirmations with respect to reasoned discourse were not illusory or fallacious; they represented an ordering of the world. Myth too represented an ordering of the world, but in reasonable discourse the ordering was of a different kind. If myth is indispensable, so is reasonable discourse. And yet many Europeans, driven by their murderous antiwestern frenzy, are endeavoring to destroy the very discourse they rely on, to rend the very word they use. They claim to be rediscovering the mythical dimension—which is sheer braggadocio; in fact, they are reducing discourse to fragments and onomatopoeic sounds in an effort to be "original," that is, to get back to the origins. They are discovering "body language" and indulging in the delirious outbursts best exemplified by Hitler.[24]

We must not fool ourselves: if we destroy reasonable language, we shall not thereby enter some wider dimension of the word, but shall find ourselves at a junction where only two paths open before us. One of them leads into the frozen world of structuralism, which reduces the word to structure and is the supreme form of rationalism. The other path is that of propaganda; it runs from Johnny Halliday[25] to Hitler, passing through Woodstock and all the "theaters of involvement" you may choose to imagine. At the moment, we are experiencing in fact a combination of the two choices. As a result, the boat in which reason is a passenger is now sinking.

For almost a century now, all the things of which we have been speaking—reason, control, coherence—have been attacked in the name of the irrational, the spontaneous, the instantaneous. The first two accusations leveled were also the most simplistic: that reason, control, and coherence were hypocrisy, and that they led to a "neurotic personality."

The "free spirits" who hated the bourgeoisie and all forms of moralism accused western man of hypocrisy—surely a moralistic judgment if ever there was one. Marx, Nietzsche, and Freud set forth their reasons for suspecting western man; they pinned him down with searchlights beamed in from different directions. The pattern of their accusations, however, was always the same: western man does not live and act according to his declared principles. Out of this grew the accusation repeated over and over in drama and literature: the moral affirmations, the proclamation of reason, the good breeding, and the seeming order are but pretenses, "rationalizations," justifications, veils hiding the reality, means of legitimizing a domination, appearances pure and simple, forms of ideology.

There was no value, truth, or sincerity in western man; on the contrary, his chief trait was duplicity. The whole construction should be torn down because in fact man really behaved in an entirely different manner. Western man claimed to be faithful to his wife, but he multiplied his adulteries; egalitarian, but he crushed the poor; liberal, but he favored those in authority; rational, but he surrendered to the desire for power; humane, but he built a world of alienation. Falsehood was everywhere.

From these premises men drew an easy conclusion, the consequences of which we are seeing today: do away with these wretched principles at which everyone in fact jeers; start being honest and authentic, with no discrepancy between being, action, and appearances. The intention was virtuous and even eminently evangelical; but the gospel is not identical with society (a fact often forgotten by the antipsychiatry movement).

To what, in fact, did the good intentions lead? Well, the only authentic model of antimorality and antiliberalism was Hitler —assuming of course that we limit ourselves to those who actually put the theory into practice and were not content simply to talk about it (like Marx or Nietzsche). Beaudelaire's fable about beating a beggar in the effort to force him to be a man is all very nice, but unless Beaudelaire actually translated the fable into practice, it was just another example of western hypocrisy. The same has to be said of the literature written to give the writer a good conscience. Merely to cast off the reins of reason does nothing to combat hypocrisy! Spontaneity, too, can be hypocritical, and the Left has nothing to show the Right by way of good example.

There is, of course, a vast difference between, on the one hand, a society that claims to obey reason, constructs a moral code, and proposes it to its members as normative, but whose members then in fact do not really follow either reason or the moral code and, on the other hand, a society that jeers at reason and gives free rein to instinct, that rejects morality so that each individual may follow his own impulses. But the latter of these two societies is not a whit more honest or authentic or liberal; it simply provides the ultimate justification for throwing off all constraints. The real difference is that on the one side you have the principle: "My actions judge me," and on the other the straightforward claim: "Anything I do is good."

A society that claims to follow reason and morality is one that stimulates self-consciousness, reflection on one's actions, and the acceptance of criticism—but such results are possible only on the basis of the principles that the society admittedly does not apply. Is anyone really unable to see the difference between the United States and Hitler or Stalin? In the United States you have the Bill of Rights, a regime that claims to be democratic and liberal, and an affirmation of respect for the person and freedom of information. In practice, you have a system that is becoming more and more a police state that practices brutality and torture, an economic and political expansion that is enslaving other peoples, and a perversion of democratic principles. As a result, the world rises in indignation and points the finger at these scandalous hypocrites.

In other words, the United States has become the whipping boy *because it has claimed to show what the face of virtue looks like!* But the very accusation is meaningless except to the extent that the principles of virtue have been publicly declared and asserted. It is precisely on the basis of the principles that the world judges the United States. These principles also play a role in the domestic life of the United States, despite the imperialist tendencies, the CIA, and the will to power. No one dares surrender fully to these tendencies or enter upon a real war or launch massive repressions, because a bad liberal and democratic conscience produced by the very principles being violated is still influential.

On the other side of the fence, Hitler and Stalin. Here you have a regime that proclaims: "The only law is the violence of the stronger, the death of the weak, a dictatorship without morality or principle; the good is identical with the state (or with the pseudo-dictatorship of the proletariat); the enemy is not a man but a lustful viper." Then, in full accord with these principles, the regime kills without remorse. What accusation will you make in the face of this? In the name of what will you assert that Stalin acted evilly? Not his own principles, for he acted in full accord with them. In the name of your own conscience? But your conscience is bourgeois, moralistic, and backward.

The only solution is not to judge such a regime and such men, but simply to attack them, as a mad dog attacks. But then, aren't you admitting that if you suppress reason and morality, you turn into a mad dog?

The same sort of thing happens within the individual. Once his "liberation" means that he ceases to pass judgment on himself, there are no longer any restraints or any reflection on his actions. Everything becomes legitimate. When you seek to suppress western hypocrisy and all "virtuous intentions," and seek instead to make your principles reflect your conduct and to make instantaneous desire the norm of the new morality, what are you doing but submitting to the law of what is materially stronger, whether it be your own strongest instinct or, in dealing with others, the one who can shout the loudest or, in dealing with society, the one with the most powerful means at his disposal?

Turn everything around and make principles the norm of action: then you have an ambiguous, unsatisfactory, and difficult situation, but there is no other way for men to be free. Freedom does not exist where brute instinct holds sway as such; all you get then is an animal existence and enslavement, as the sad doings at Saint-Germain in the seventies show. Freedom exists when reason makes its demands and man can-

not fulfill them completely. And the paths to this freedom are
the effective consciousness of what one is and does, reflection
on this consciousness, and self-criticism, whereas the refusal
of these requirements means a regression to the lowest kind
of socio-animal determinism. Moreover, the ancient reflex
whereby the western man of today levels the charge of hypocrisy against the western man of yesterday is itself a manifestation of freedom and a proclamation of the moral demands
inherent in freedom. The very accusation of hypocrisy is a
direct product of the freedom that western man alone has
achieved. But there has been a sea change. When Jesus called
the scribes and Pharisees hypocrites, he was challenging them
to live up to the principles they proclaimed. At the present
time, the same accusation is nothing but an attempt at self-
justification, an excuse for abandoning principles.

A further point for consideration: you may accuse good
breeding of hypocrisy, but is it not clear that when manners
oblige a person to conceal his envious feelings, when they
drop a kind of protective veil between two persons, and when
they forbid the use of certain words, they keep human relations from being marred by violence and intolerance? By re-
pressing certain of my impulses, good breeding forces me to
stand off and take the time needed for determining exactly
what I should do, and thus for establishing a viable relation
with another person. Psychoanalysis and Sartrism are making
us more and more aware that the other person represents a
deadly danger to us. The "primitives" who codified human
relations were well aware of this danger and did not need
metaphysics to tell them about it. They established the rituals
and, later, the codes of manners that were required to eliminate the danger or reduce it to a tolerable level. When the
young of today in their virtuous indignation reject good manners and good breeding, they act as ignorant fools.

The second great accusation was that reason, control, and
coherence lead to the "neurotic personality." Surely, everyone
knows how the explanation runs: western society teaches its
little children humility, virtue, justice, love of neighbor, and

truthfulness; but when the children who have assimilated these teachings grow up and go out into the world, what do they see? They see lies and injustice triumphant, unrestrained competition making its way by crushing the weak, dishonesty successful, and virtue scorned. If a person wants to succeed (or merely not lose ground) in this kind of society, he must do the exact opposite of the principles which that society teaches him and all its young. The result is mental confusion in the individual, or even a breakdown of personality that finds expression in neuroses.

This is really the same accusation all over again, but on the medical and psychological rather than the moral level. In reply, we must ask whether such breakdowns are not the price to be paid so that society may not be even worse than it is; so that human evolution may be rendered possible by the tension between the demands made and the difficulty of meeting them; and so that freedom may be constantly reborn. Freedom exists only in the conflict between the call to be, to be born, and to grow, and the objections to this call, the response to which is hindered by the obstacles that must be surmounted.

In the name of freedom we must turn the challenge around: "You say: 'If a person wants to succeed in this kind of society, he must be dishonest.' But is success so important? And is not the criterion of success very questionable?" If you are not driven by a desire to succeed, freedom becomes far more accessible; the interplay between the requirements of reason and the social context, and the exercise of freedom cease to be hampered by the conditions laid down by "success."

The whole notion of freedom being exercised amid conflict is, as we said before, a product of western man. To apply the idea in real life requires great effort, of course, and not everyone is up to meeting the challenge. Men die or are wounded in the ever new struggle for freedom. Some people cannot support the tension, the conflict, and they become neurotics (at least, that *may* be the cause of their neuroses; but remember, there are many other causes of neuroses, not least among those who claim to be liberated from their "complexes" and "inhibitions").

On the other hand, contradiction and conflict are necessary if we are to be able to evolve, if we are to be called to move beyond our present stage. Evidently, we must be rather solidly rooted and capable of putting up resistance. This presents us with another aspect of western man: he is shaped by demands that are beyond his strength; he is challenged to transcend himself (in an act of transcending that is just as valuable as the self-transcendence effected by drugs). He does what no animal is capable of doing: he is challenged, and he challenges himself. Sometimes he meets the challenge, sometimes it is too much for him.

Western man forces himself to live amid contradiction, and by that fact discovers new and hitherto unknown paths. Contradiction, whether he seeks to master it, or whether he flees from it, forces him to discover and invent, control things and himself. Inevitably, the weakest succumb and sink into neuroses, but it is impossible to strike out on the complicated paths of freedom without running the risk of succumbing to the various "mental alienations"—the neuroses and psychoses, the paranoias and the deliriums—that are the antitype of freedom. In order to avoid these dangers, shall we abandon the struggle with contradiction, the rigorous demands of reason and morality? If we do, from then on all we shall hear is vague rumblings like those we hear in a swamp when bubbles of gas form below and burst with a dull hollow sound at the surface, attesting a bottomless corruption. All that will be left of the real human being will be a stagnant surface covered with slimy rotting moss, a spot where someone has fallen into the mire and not emerged again, a clammy malodorous tranquillity, and the only motion will be that of a gigantic digestive system.

Hatred of reason, hatred of its strict demands—does that represent a return to nature? That is what we are constantly being told. Western man is regarded as being antinatural because he has branded as unnatural sexual habits that dogs, for example, find perfectly natural. He is accused of being antinatural because he has so greatly differentiated himself from what we consider to be "natural man." There is a new upsurge of "primitivism" today, imitating that of Rousseau long ago or of D. H. Lawrence in the twenties.

This time, the phenomenon of primitivism is more complicated because it is associated with the condemnation of colonialism and imperialism. People reject the norms and reason and morality of western man and hope to prove by doing so that they have gone over to the other side: the side of those who have been wiped out, the side of the Indians and blacks who have been conquered and exploited and oppressed. Rarely, however does the "going over" amount to anything more than the assertion of "sexual freedom"; people dress up as Indians, gypsies, Chinese, Hindus, or Eskimos, but the whole thing has a carnival air about it. Really, not even a carnival air, for a carnival is funny and amusing and full of gaiety, good humor, and fantasy, whereas when we meet these fellows disguised as non-Westerners we find ourselves in a world that is deadly serious, heavy, grim, accusatory, aggressive, armor-clad in a "good conscience," and filled with hatred. The disguise guarantees the legitimacy of the judgment these people pass on others!

By abandoning both western dress and reason, these people think they are aligning themselves with the poor and oppressed and are recovering a truly natural authenticity. Primitive man is still causing a lot of harm! But surely we must at least remind ourselves at this point that no one believes any longer that the savage is a primitive or that the primitive is in a "state of nature." No matter how far back we go and no matter how "primitive" the people the ethnologist studies, he finds that every human group obeys a detailed code of regulations, prescriptions, and ordinances. There is no "state of nature," no spontaneous behavior; everywhere there are statutes, hierarchies, and codes.

As a matter of fact, it was western man who challenged all these statutes and hierarchies and codes! Consequently, when our splendid young revolutionaries turn away in anger from western rationality, they are simply doing what the western world which they reject and flee has been doing for two thousand years! Are they ashamed of the West? Good, let them change it and move it forward. But no one has yet found a better means of doing this than the means we now possess. What is needed is to make even greater demands, not to live a life without constraints; to be even more strict, not to crawl back into the maternal womb.

How very odd and delusory these great urges to primitiveness and "nature" are can be seen from the ways and means chosen to implement them. Sexual inconstancy, a glut of sexual experiences, drugs, disguises—how much more artificial, complicated, and antinatural can you be?[26] The claims to free a man's inner impulses through drugs, or, at the other extreme, to rise above the human condition through planning are as antinatural as the cultivation of one's inner energies in order to transcend oneself (a very western notion!). The further claim that we thereby return to primitive ways is to forget that we are, quite simply, no longer primitives, and that we have no choice about being or not being primitives. You cannot erase twenty-five-hundred years in a decade! Timothy Leary's "way" is nothing but a form of western sophistication. You cannot return to your sources.

The whole array of narcotics and other drugs is, then, nothing but a further form of disguise, a further layer added to the sedimentary strata in western man. There are two things that prevent them from being anything else. One is that in the traditional societies hallucinogenics met precise needs which are no longer ours (in our society they are merely ways of coping with boredom or getting "experiences"). The other is that in the traditional societies the use of these drugs fitted into the social framework, as means, for example, of achieving an altered state of consciousness; but for us today they lead simply to a fragmentation of our lives. There is no real likeness and nothing in common between the use of drugs in those bygone worlds and the use of drugs in our world. By no stretch of the imagination do we return through drugs to a primitive or natural state. We simply take a step even further away from nature, and, in so doing, we stray from the royal way the West has opened for us, and we gain nothing in its place. Drugs are simply a form of suicide.

The same must be said for disguising ourselves as Indians

or other peoples. This is really a thoroughly western idea and results, once again, from the process of criticism and challenge we have initiated. In this case, however, the criticism turns its back on itself. The disguise is a denial of the self, but does not enable the person to find himself in an other. We may refuse to be ourselves, but do we become Lapps by wearing Eskimo boots (in midsummer, of course) or even by smearing ourselves with seal oil? Of course not! We reject something, but we do not change anything. If the whole business does not end in suicide, it becomes simply ridiculous.

At the present time, the hatred of reason has come up with a new charge: the West is blamed for rejecting the madman. Reason has committed the unpardonable crime of labeling the madman and then excluding him from society. Admittedly, the triumph of reason in our society has been so great that everything which is not rational must be eliminated, and the madman, after all, is the enemy who questions the primacy of reason.

Things are not quite that simple. The history of western society's dealings with the mad has passed through several stages, and it is not at all clear that reason as such is to blame for the modern treatment of madmen. In traditional societies, as everyone knows, the mad person shares in the life of the social body; he is not shunted aside, still less is he locked up. He has his recognized place and can get along quite easily on what other people give him. His utterances and his behavior are considered to be the result of possession, but there are two kinds of possession. There are fortunate possessions that allow the madman to live his life and also to communicate messages from the gods or express some aspect of the sacred. There are also unfortunate possessions in which demons are at work, making the madman a danger to everyone else or driving him to suicide. In this second type of possession, society believes an effort must be made to cure the person. We have a fine example of this in the Gospels when Jesus cures the madmen who live in tombs in the country of the Gadarenes.

Even in Greece, in the period when reason was exalted, there was no change in society's attitude to the mad. Or at

Rome, where the mad were subject to civil limitations (they could not engage in juridically valid acts), they were neither locked up nor excluded from society. (This despite what Foucault says in his history of madness.[27] His book is a compendium of historical errors, and should have been called "The Romance of Madness According to Foucault." To the historian his method and his use of information are unacceptable.) The same attitude persists throughout the Middle Ages. Christianity does not exclude the madman; neither does the quest for rationality.

This much is true, however: as men became more and more clearly conscious of their action, the coherence of personality and discourse and the rationality of behavior became increasingly important; to that extent the madman became a marginal figure. Not entirely marginal indeed, for we all know the role played by the fool in the royal courts (a very ancient tradition, preserved to the end of the western Middle Ages). The madman in this case was a person to whom everything was permitted precisely because he was mad (the opposite of the nineteenth-century approach to the matter). He could say anything he wanted to the king; he could even accuse him of anything and everything. But his words were charged with a profound ambiguity: he could say whatever he wanted because his words, being irrational, were unimportant, but also because his words came from depths that were sacred, and therefore were inspired by some obscure but radical power which ordinary men could not resist and which communicated to his words a suprarational truth.

The role of the madman or fool in the royal court was a reflection of his role in society at large and in relation to the social body as a whole. The situation changed once the centralized political power became an embodiment of reason, and once "rational science" became the great manifestation of reason. Once the whole of society was concentrated, as it were, in a single sovereign individual and later in a government, and once everything had to pass the scrutiny of science and rational technique, there could no longer be any place for the madman; he had to move to the periphery of society.

We should note, furthermore, that the triumph of democracy brought a considerable worsening of the madman's position. A king by divine right could allow himself to have in his court a fool who might ridicule him; he was so superior, so assured of his power, that the insults were tolerable and he could converse with the fool. The president of a republic, on the other hand, is a frail being; he wears no aura of majesty and possesses no innate superiority. Therefore he cannot allow his dignity to be diminished; he needs all the formalities and honors and signs of greatness, because the substance of greatness is not there. A grimacing fool has no place at a president's side, whereas he was natural counterpart of a king.

I must qualify these remarks somewhat. From the communist point of view, what I have just been saying is incorrect, because the state and the science in question were bourgeois, and it was the bourgeoisie that excluded madmen from their midst. (People think that by qualifying the state and the science as "bourgeois" they have made an amazing discovery and indeed are real geniuses. In fact, the word "bourgeois" simply serves as a means of lining themselves up on the right side, of gaining a good conscience, of denying any responsibility, and of having a simple reassuring explanation for things. In other words, using the term "bourgeois" is just a rationalization of their situation.) I agree with the communist claim if it means that the bourgeoisie carried the concern for rationality to extremes and fell into rationalism. This is really to say, however, that the fact that people were bourgeois was not the important thing; it was the state and the use of rational technique that determined the nature of the bourgeoisie, and not vice versa.[28]

The important thing, then, was the historical direction of the forces at work; the bourgeoisie was simply the agent of those forces for the time being. To believe that the bourgeoisie made the modern world what it is is like believing the myth that earthquakes are due to the movement of the tortoise on whose back the globe rests. The bourgeoisie did indeed exclude the madman from society and lock him up, but the bourgeoisie simply happened to be the ones who carried rationality to extremes, applied it to everything, and could not endure

any form of irrationality. As everyone knows, in socialist societies, no less than in bourgeois societies, madmen are excluded from society, locked up, and put in chains.

Let me ask: Where did the protest against the exclusion of
the mad originate? Where did the antipsychiatry movement
make its appearance? In the capitalist West, among the intellectuals of the West, and specifically among bourgeois intellectuals: men who are the sons of the bourgeois, the grandsons
of the bourgeois, themselves bourgeois to their fingertips, new
incarnations of bourgeois intellectual liberalism, representatives of bourgeois rational science. (They adhere to a different
interpretative ideology, it is true, but the ideology itself
emerged from the bourgeoisie. What greater proof do you
need that the whole business is a matter of ideology, not of
class?) The proletariat had no finger in this pie at all. The
urban proletariat has no soft spot for madmen, and sees no
reason why they should not be locked up.

In any case, this lengthy discussion was meant simply to
bring before the reader the charges presently being leveled
against the West in the name of the madman. According to the
moving discourses pronounced by the antipsychiatrists, the
madman is a product of western society. He is the sign of its
guilt and of the remorse it should feel, the living proof that it
is a lying, disturbed society. It is the society that is mad, not
the "madman," who is simply trying to be authentically human
and whose discourse seems incoherent only because the "coherence" of society is the result of a mad, blinkered logic.

I would agree with this diagnosis, provided I may add that
our technical society is not a true expression of the West but
its betrayal; that what society manifests is not reason but a
raving rationalism. It is precisely here that the (justified) defenders of the madman make no distinction. For them, wisdom
is no longer to be found in study that is guided by reason and
in thought that is subject to reason, but in the verbal outbursts
of the wandering mind. If we take Artaud in his final stage, he
ends up supplanting Pascal. In the name of the madman who
has been excluded, people reject not the structures that led to
the exclusion (the state and rationalistic science), but the ac-

tion and discourse of reason, which they regard as terrorist activities bent on mutilating man.

Reason certainly involves making choices, but can you live without making choices? And is not the choice in favor of the madman an act of reason? Moreover, if the madman were thrust out into the world of nature and left to his own resources, would he survive? If man did not from the beginning behave in ways that were not mad, would there be any humankind at all? If you tell me that all that is unimportant, then please do not plead with me in behalf of the mad, the imprisoned, the starving, the proletariat, for then there is nothing important about those conditions either.

The madman is not the embodiment of some objective metaphysical truth or some truth about man and the depths of man's being. The madman's discourse is unimportant except in relation to reason and within a world marked by reason; only there does he become meaningful. Statist and technical rationalism may have felt obliged to exclude the madman, but reason itself has never ceased to heed the words of the mad; it knows itself to be involved in a dialogue with the mad and to exist in tension with them. The activity of reason is not a monomaniacal development that is closed off and excludes everything else. To condemn reason in the name of the madman's rights is to destroy the only power that can give the madman his authentic place. But the exalted fervor in behalf of the mad, like the fervor in behalf of the primitive, is completely blind; it is ready moreover to inflict any and every mutilation, provided only it may in a bloody rage destroy the hideous Westerners who are the cause of all evil!

Even in the face of such an attitude as that, we cannot but raise this question: Why, and in the name of what, is it more human to give oneself over to one's instincts and passions than deliberately and firmly to build up a human type that is marked by reason and self-control, namely, western man? Passions and instincts are surely basic, but are they, in the last analysis, what makes man man? If you submit purely and simply to "sexual energy" (poor Wilhelm Reich's *orgone*), are you then a man?[29] If you adopt behavior that has to be justified by the claim that it is natural because (supposedly) comparable to the behavior of animals, are you then a man? Does being a man mean being identical with the animals or being different?

For a long time, the whole emphasis was on the difference between man and the animals (and the assertion was made in a rather arrogant spirit). Today, the pendulum has swung. And yet, in no spirit of outraged pride, we are forced to recognize that what is specific to man is connected with the differentiation of his activity from directly animal behavior. Ritualization is no longer the same in man and in brute; above all, symbolization is peculiar to man. In fact, the people now throwing down the gauntlet to reason and to the type of human being represented by western man would be utterly at a loss if they had to give up symbolization. Yet this simple truth never enters their heads!

Symbolization in turn leads to the discovery of reason, for there is no necessary opposition between reason and the world of myth.

The new proclamation that man must follow his instincts and that mental disturbance takes priority over sanity means a deadly regression to the time before man became man. As I have often said before, man became man, not when he asserted his superiority to the other species nor when he threw his first stone, but when he formulated the rule, "You shall not kill." That moment marked the beginning of humanness, the beginning of reason, the beginning of self-control.

How, moreover, is man possibly to be completely unartificial and remain man? The prehistorians consider the bones they discover to be certainly human when they are found together with some sort of tools; the invention of tools, that is, artificial means of achieving results, accompanies man and assures his continued existence. It is by his contradiction to nature in general as much as to his own nature that we recognize man. He builds an artificial world, he is an artificer, he lives with the help of artifacts; he has no other means of asserting himself as a man and of developing as a man. If, then, this deliberate, steady construction of a whole world finds expression in the construction of man himself, how can we claim this is treason and inhuman, and that only a return to some primitive state will save man?

That is nonsense. Reason and self-control—inventions of the West—are the highest form of man's self-discovery. Never before or elsewhere has man so completely realized his own potentialities or reached such a summit or been so fulfilled. But at the same time never has there been so great a danger of a two-fold collapse. One failure would be to retreat and regress because it seems impossible to live under such tension and to meet the demands of self-control (this is the collapse to which the flabbiness of our neo-leftists will lead). The other would be to succumb to the madness induced by rationalized power (this is the demon that drives a technicized society). The West has created the best and produced the worst, because man cannot permanently maintain so difficult and demanding a balance.

Reason and self-control: but let us not forget the context in which these are to be placed. They are, as we have pointed out at some length, restraints indispensable for the development of freedom. The man who is free with the conscious deliberate freedom for which the West stands cannot be a man of utter spontaneity, a man utterly unfettered. The second-rate heroes of comic opera are not free at any point; they are puppets on a string. Freedom that is uncontrolled becomes material for the playwright. On the other hand, psychological and social conditioning has been critically analyzed and gradually eliminated; natural barriers have been overcome by the application of rational methods. Western man thus has the means for achieving total control, despite the fact that he is heir to the great discovery of freedom.

The consequence of all this is that the whole human enterprise is in danger unless freedom itself is subjected to control. That is the point we were making when we insisted that reason and self-control are the means of using freedom properly. If we reject these means, what will the result be? We must not delude ourselves here. The result will not be a purely anarchic society marked by a glorious spontaneity. The social body reacts like a biological organism, and produces antitoxins. If society is challenged and endangered by what professes to be absolute freedom, it will replace the unsuccessful internal constraints with external constraints, and the latter will be the more rigorous as the double threat of unrestrained power and unrestrained freedom is the more serious. This brings us back to Lorenz's theory on aggressivity: if there are no internal restraints, then external barriers must be constructed. If the force in question is a powerful one, then the restraints will have to be rigorously effective. Is not that precisely the ultimate explanation for modern dictatorships?

When freedom claims to be unconditional, when men deny the value of reason and plunge into the delights of the senses, and when the means of action pile up, then there is no way of preventing collective suicide but a dictatorship. The only things that can prevent the growth of fascisms are reason and the acceptance of strict personal self-control, and a concern for strict and clearcut conduct, for permanent self-criticism, for internal coherence, and for uncompromisingly critical rational discourse. These procedures are by no means the product of a muscular voluntarism of the extreme right, nor defense mechanisms employed by a shifty bourgeoisie in behalf of its selfish interests.

As a matter of fact, only occasionally are capitalist groups of a fascist or Machiavellian character the agents by which society reacts strongly when the restraints upon aggressivity are destroyed. The real cause of the growth of fascism, the people who make the appearance of fascism inevitable, are the frenzied people of every kind: the sexists, the irrationalists, the primitivists, those who with touching naïveté believe they are defending the freedom of the Women's Liberation Movement or the Coalition for the Defense of Homosexuals, when in fact they are directly preparing for, begetting, and nourishing fascism. The muddle-headed leftists confuse freedom with aggressiveness; they think in ready-made categories: class struggle, repression, genocide, etc., thus making a mishmash of everything under the pretext that "the system has the power to recover"; they think they are radical because their language is as mixed up as it is violent. However, their good will and their good intentions will vanish like a mist when the wind blows. But it is they themselves whose emptiness and rhetoric summon the wind to blow. Nor will it be a purifying wind; it will bring with it what may prove to be the final ice age, the ultimate denial of our society, of the West.

3 Mystery of the West

A current cliché has it that the West was born of the union between Greek thought, Roman order, and the Christian movement. This is simply taken for granted. The historians and the essayists repeat it without raising an eyebrow, without asking any questions—as though Greek thought, Roman order, and Christianity were layers that could be fitted to each other and superimposed on each other, and as though their union were completely unproblematic.

It can certainly be said that historically and sheerly as a matter of fact this union and superimposition, even this fusion, did take place, although we can hardly speak of it as a synthesis. What people forget is the price that was paid for the union. What price? Greek thought completely distorted, falsified, and misappropriated by Christian theologians and philosophers; Roman order and power ruined by Christianity, then recouped and reorganized in barbaric terms and ways; Christianity secularized by contact with Roman politics and law, then completely perverted by contact with Greek philosophy.

No, the intermingling was by no means to be taken for granted, nor can it said that the outcome was a happy one. The components were in fact contradictory each to the others. The contradiction is even clearer if we think of Christianity not as a religious system or a semiphilosophical system of thought or as a moral code, but as the revelation of God in Jesus Christ. We must have the courage to admit that the elements which met and mixed were not meant to go together, that the forces which joined hands were in fact opposed to one another.

The mystery of history since Jesus Christ (and we may say,

of all human history, if we really take Jesus Christ seriously) is
that it was in the West that Christianity developed and revelation was broadcast. For, the West is, in itself, the opposite of
what God teaches us and bids us live in Christ. The mystery
of the West is that, for twenty centuries now, it has felt the pull
of two strictly contradictory factors which, for all its efforts and
betrayals and compromises, it has never been able to bring
into unity, balance, and order. In my book *Hope in Time of
Abandonment*[30] I thought it worth exploring this contradiction
because the contemporary situation in the West is making
clear, as never before, the contradiction between the two directions being followed; the seeming unity as well as the greatness that did in fact issue from the brittle synthesis are today
being subjected to a deadly challenge.

How was the Mediterranean world to be described? The
Greek mind had plumbed the depths of man. Never before had
so much intellectual acumen, so much bold yet rigorous thinking, been deliberately brought to bear by a large number of
individuals. Everything was subjected to analysis: the city and
the world, gods and men, virtue and value, ethics and metaphysics; all the ways of thinking, from systematic philosophy
to passionate involvement, from cold objectivity to concrete
application, from the Socratic to the dogmatic; all the modes
of syllogistic reasoning; all the schools, all the possible interpretations, all the modes of thought, all the objects of thought
—and this in an incredibly short period of time.

Myth had expressed what the rational mind could not formulate. The world of the gods and the world of men were now
clearly distinguished and objectively explained. No bold advance was unthinkable, and the very gods were suddenly dethroned, reduced in rank, and made means to an end. In a way
never paralleled anywhere before, triumphant reason could
calmly assert its superiority to these empty shadows and assign
them a role as actors on a stage built by reason itself. There
was nothing this mind could not boast of successfully undertaking.

Everything was cut down to size, with man as the only absolute; everything was now measured by man: the perfectly har-

monious, gorgeous, but empty-eyed man we see in Greek stat-
uary. This man of reason was not alone, but was accompanied
by a retinue of grimacing masks which were also man, but man
in another dimension, man seen from another perspective.
Monsters were never absent from the scene, for they, too, were
a necessary part of the vision of the human world. Like the
gods, they had lost their existence apart, their autonomy, their
hidden depths, and had been cut down to man's size; they had
become myths of man's anxiety and of the dark forces that
dwell in him, driving him but also possessed by him. Intelligence had laid claim to everything that was thinkable.

Then came Rome, the other pole of the same tendency and
the same will. Rome, too, dominated and organized, but this
time in a different order of being, that of the political and the
human "exterior." The modern expert on ancient Rome is
irritated by the description, or better the two opposing descriptions which political essayists or pseudo-historians give of
Roman history and the Roman adventure. On the one hand,
we see a Rome based on slavery, a Rome that is the expression
of class struggle and dominates the world through military
terror, a vile and hypocritical Rome that exploits the nations
and reduces the subject peoples to wretchedness. On the other
hand, we find the exact opposite: a glorious Rome, mother of
arts, arms, and laws, a Rome that establishes a centuries-long
peace, leads peoples to their adulthood, and builds an orderly
existence which had never been seen before and which others
later on would try in vain to reproduce, a Rome that in its
concern for justice creates law and a marvelously balanced
constitutional system. But both images are simply propaganda, the first Marxist, the second Roman; both are false and
inadequate.

The truth of Rome is not to be found in these descriptions.
We can indeed stand amazed that with so small an army Rome
could not only conquer her empire but preserve it and introduce order into its incoherent parts. The Romans certainly
showed a political, juridical, and administrative genius never
matched elsewhere. If Greece is the high point of philosophy,
Rome is the high point of the political. Everything that can be
said and done in the political, administrative, and juridical

spheres was said and done at Rome: subtle balances; juridical inventions that were applied concretely and sufficed to make political justice coexist with order; constant renewal of institutions, not by an absurd proliferation of new ones but by a development of the old ones to fit new situations; the invention of the overall concept of the state (an invention that determined the political destiny of the West); broadening of participation in the popular will; assertion of the superiority of law over the ruler's will; etc.

The essential point to be grasped, however, is that Greece and Rome were part of the same movement, that each in its own sphere obeyed the same inspiration. The driving force was Eros. I have no hesitation about adopting Nygren's contrast between Eros and Agape, despite the criticisms to which it has been subjected, and despite the fact that we may question the accuracy of characterizing Eros as possessive, tenacious love that seeks to take for itself and dominate.[31] This Eros may, in the final analysis, be closer to the Freudian eros than is often believed. It is love as a conquering passion that gains ascendancy over man. And even if, as I am willing to believe, the Greek thinkers saw more to Eros than that, the term is nevertheless a handy one for labeling a certain attitude to life. Nygren may not have succeeded in recovering the correct meaning of the word itself, but he did assign it a meaning that is quite useful as well as historically valid for describing the human attitude we find embodied by Rome and Athens.

What was that attitude? The will to power. Athens sought intellectual domination; explanation that admitted no limits to the reach of the spirit; control of gods and men; here was Eros that seeks eagerly to possess in the world of the mind. Rome sought political domination; the establishment of an order that acknowledged neither geographical nor social nor economic limits; juridical control of gods and men: the possessive Eros at work in the political sphere. Here is where the greatness and the hidden thrust of Athens and Rome is to be found. In an astonishingly short period of time, man succeeded in creating a focus for Eros in its entirety, and bringing it to bear upon the whole of the human condition.

For the first time, man found the way to exalt himself; or, in ethical terms, man's pride found expression at every level and had at last taken shape in far more complete and satisfying ways than the old ways of Egypt and Chaldea. The world of Greece and Rome was indeed a world in which everything was reduced to man and everything was made to contribute to the glorification of man. Two royal roads were discovered for suddenly humanizing all things; these two roads have never since been abandoned.

Into this world the gospel was to be carried, the gospel that was in utter, open, irreducible contradiction to it. The myth of Babel now turned into history. In the intellectual and political spheres man had built a world that was as exclusively and completely human as any world could be, and now God said, "Come, let us go down and see. . . ." It is as though God were determined to install contradiction at the very heart of man's claims to greatness. For, in fact, he was about to introduce into the universe of Eros its direct opposite, Agape.

From that moment, the West was launched upon a strange career, for Eros possessed it more than any other area of the world, dominated it more than any other civilization, and yet at the same time the West was brutally invaded by the very opposite of Eros and chosen to become bearer of the revelation of Agape. The West has never managed to recover from this contradiction; it has carried a poisoned, incurable wound. It travels its own peculiar road, that of Eros, but it cannot do so with a sense of triumph or the feeling that it is acting wisely or in good conscience. It exalts its own accomplishments but must bow down under its self-accusations. It attempts impossible syntheses of the two forces at work in it, and each time it betrays the one or the other.

The West has therefore been permanently deformed; it is sick and powerless to be itself. God has as it were breached the solid wall of its success and self-exaltation, and the breach has never been closed. It has been said with some justification that Christianity has been the sickness of the West;[32] of course, accepting such an analysis means admitting that the will to power is health. In any case, we are confronted with two utterly contradictory and irreconcilable powers, and the history of the

West is the history of their opposition. From the Christian point of view and in accordance with what the Scriptures tell us about the pattern God follows in his decrees, the opposition means that he has intervened once again precisely at the point where man reaches the pinnacle of his power and autonomy.

If this be indeed the structure of western history, we may say that the decisive moment occurred on the night when God in a dream ordered Paul to cross the straits into Greece. As the Acts of the Apostles tells it: "And a vision appeared to Paul in the night: a man of Macedonia was standing beseeching him and saying, 'Come over to Macedonia and help us.' And when he had seen the vision, immediately we sought to go on into Macedonia, concluding that God had called us to preach the gospel to them" (Acts 16:9–10). Upon this vision the specific character of western civilization depends; at this moment the mystery peculiar to the West and the contradiction that runs through western history come into being.

Imagine Christianity expanding toward the East instead of toward the West. The result? Western history would have been radically different, proving that all the major historical events were secondary in comparison with Paul's dream. If the Persians instead of the Greeks had won at Marathon or Salamis, western civilization would not have been different. If Caesar had not been assassinated or Augustus had lost or Alexander had lived to old age or had been conquered instead of conquering, nothing of importance would have changed in the history of the world. Different details perhaps, different people running things; speedups and slowdowns at other moments in the sequence: in other words, all the ordinary variations of historical events.

If, however, the Mediterranean world had remained pagan, had developed according to its native genius, and had expanded under Germanic auspices, how differently the West would have turned out! The course of history would have been radically altered if the western will to power had been given free rein, unhindered by a bad conscience. The Middle Ages would have been different, and so would capitalism. Paul's vision was thus the crucial moment for western civilization. It was the moment when God took radical action in the political and intellectual spheres.

I do not speak here of the action of "providence," for God is not a providence. His actions in history, moreover, are rare and hidden. Paul's dream is typical of God's action: Paul is summoned by a vision to preach the gospel; he is asked for help by a man who seeks salvation. It is thus a decision that refers only to *preaching* and to the proclamation of *salvation,* that will determine the course of history far more than all the struggles between the political parties of the day, far more than the great men and the modes of production. God changed the course of history and politics and society and civilization by means of a vision that had nothing to do with history or politics or society or civilization. He introduced another dimension into the works of man; these works are surely indispensible, but they reveal their deepest meaning only in response to the challenge issued by God.

For these reasons I regard the usual explanations based on divine providence as incorrect. Some historians and theologians say, for example, that the reason Christianity was able to spread so rapidly was because Rome had unified the then known world. To some interpreters, this explanation is a purely rational one. To others, it is proof that providence was secretly at work in history, enabling Rome to conquer the world so that the gospel might be spread. Neither explanation takes into account the very great extent to which Greco-Roman civilization, which at every point was diametrically opposed to the gospel, was an obstacle to its spread. The unification of the empire was as nothing (except in terms of physical communication, i.e., land routes and sea lanes) when compared with the contradiction to the gospel that was inherent in the spirit of the empire.

It is idle speculation, then, for materialists to think that a universal empire must have a universal religion, or for the spiritually minded to think that the Roman empire played a prophetic role and paved the way for "him who was to come." Exactly the opposite was the case. The logical course would have been for Christianity to spread eastward. Everything sug-

gested the advisability of this. To proclaim a spiritual religion
in the homeland of spiritual religions would have been to
guarantee a favorable reception. To preach a resurrected God
in countries that were quite at home with dying and rising gods
would have been to speak the language of the place.[33]

If, then, a group of men wanted to proclaim salvation
through the death of their God, they would automatically have
been given a favorable reception in the East. Just think, moreover, of how well the disciples would have been received just
beyond the frontiers by Rome's ever restless enemies, the
Parthians, if they had gone as representatives of a founder
whom the Romans had put to death! The Parthians would
have regarded them as fellow victims of a common enemy and
therefore as allies. If the disciples had then gone even further
east, they would have found Asiatic peoples whose Buddhism
would have shown their openness to the things of the spirit.

Everything, therefore, absolutely everything—cultural climate, psychological readiness, political situation—urged the
first Christians to turn to the East. Yet they went in the opposite direction! Was this a simple error on the part of the disciples? Were they yielding to the sociological pressures that
impelled everything and everybody toward Rome? Did they
decide, being Jews, to follow the paths of the Jewish Diaspora
throughout the Mediterranean basin? This last consideration
may have played some part in the decision, but in the last
analysis I think the answer is that God was determined to enter
into the lists at the very center of man's power, the place where
his ambition and pride and will to power were most fully
embodied and most clearly manifested.

It seems to me that no rational pattern is to be seen in the
movement of Christianity into the empire. If, then, we look for
some sociological, economic, psychological, or philosophical
compatibility between this development and the structures of
the empire, we condemn ourselves to understand nothing. We
plunge into a maze from which Christianity has never succeeded in emerging when we try to use what contradicts Christianity as a way of explaining the development of Christianity;
when we attempt the famous synthesis of the gospel and Greek

philosophy or the gospel and Roman law; when we try to make Eros and Agape compatible partners. We can see the "new theologies" making the same attempt today with exemplary patience (except that this time Eros is chiefly a political and economic force).

Our only chance of understanding what happened is to accept that there was an irreducible contradiction between Christianity, on the one hand, and, on the other, the socio-cultural situation in the empire and in the civilization that succeeded it. Once we accept this, however, we are faced with a mind-boggling fact: the West whose whole spirit and every work bore the mark of dionysiac Eros was chosen by God as bearer of the revelation of Anti-Eros or Agape! The West was chosen to bear witness to the gift of self amid the lust for possession, to self-humbling amid the quest for power, to the Spirit amid a world of rigid structures, to freedom amid a civilization shot through with rationalism. It is precisely here that we have the great dramatic conflict of the West. The West has never been able to reach its logical end because it was pierced to the heart by a gospel that was its utter opposite and constantly undermined all its grandiose projects. Christianity, on the other hand, has never been able to be fully itself because it has been tangled in a network of systems that have constantly been endeavoring to assimilate it.

The greatness of the West, then, consists in this, that it is the place where God has issued his final and most radical challenge to man, because it is the place where man has attained his own greatest stature. We are confronted by the challenge God issued in response to man's challenge. Christianity is the testimony to an Other Love and was proclaimed when man had renounced love for the sake of power. Nor did God fight man with man's own weapons; he did not come clad in the power of the One who had caused the confusion at Babel or who had unleashed the deluge. Instead, he attempted to penetrate to the center, the heart, the root of the whole conflict; he attempted to go back and make the whole human adventure start all over again, so that its course might be entirely different. Once God had thus chosen the place and direction, the conflict was engaged. The West became the site of the most radical kind of spiritual combat. All the works and creations, all the political, intellectual, economic, and technical advances of the West have been the result of this tension and conflict, this constant head-on collision between man who wants to be himself and God who also wants man to be himself. The difficulty is that "himself" does not mean the same thing in both cases; in fact, the one meaning contradicts the other.

What of the present moment? In my view we have in our day reached the climax of all the tension and conflict and contradiction. In the last two centuries the West has taken a giant step in the direction pointed out by philosophical and political Eros. Hitherto we had had the ambition, the proud desire to follow Eros; we had wanted power and domination, we had wanted to create ourselves as human beings, but we had few of the means needed. Now, however, while rejecting God (mankind rejects him even when it assimilates him, makes a social convention of him, makes him the object of a sociological religion and the corrupted inspiration of ideologies and political creeds), man has reached a decisive turning point: he has acquired the means to satisfy his Eros and his arrogant pride. In the ongoing conflict, men dealt deceitfully with God and rendered his revelation sterile by snaring it in the lime of Scholastic cleverness and political lies. Now man finds himself suddenly provided with means so powerful that it seems he need no longer try to trick the enemy. Instead, he can launch a frontal attack and, for practical purposes, eliminate everything that revelation had sought to introduce along the way of man's self-exaltation.

Today man seems to be completely in control. The intellectual weapon he uses in attempting to destroy the enemy is no longer the ineffective weapon of philosophy. It is science, a tool that enables him to implement his desire for complete rationality, and that satisfies every test of intellectual rigor while also lending itself to effective application. Man is at last able to do what the prophets had said was impossible: he can radically change God's work and modify the conditions of human life and even the very being of man himself, as well as nature throughout its whole extent. He can annihilate; he can cause matter to be transformed into energy (he can perhaps even effect an anticreation); he can create new matter. He is becoming like the God who supposedly created the universe. At the same time, he has the means of transforming human psychology and human culture.

God is not only becoming the useless hypothesis, the stop-gap. His gospel is no longer the gospel that exalts suffering, the freedom of the Spirit, the gift of self, the practice of giving without seeking a return. When the "gospel of the poor" is preached today, the purpose is to rouse the poor to rebellion, violence, and hatred. That is, the aim is to set them on the path of Eros and pride! Man no longer needs to proceed by trickery, to take the roundabout way or use pretexts to attempt to assimilate the gospel revelation. He has no need of all this now, because he has won; he has proved himself the stronger. Greco-Roman Eros has at last triumphed in our day through the general application of rationality and through the univer-salization of the political. The humble, dying God who was handed over into the power of men has at last been conquered and almost eliminated. The Agape he brought into the world has been completely domesticated. It still exists, but there is no need of referring it any longer to the God who gave it to men, for it has been integrated into man's political system.

There is no doubt that Jesus was crucified in about the seven hundred and seventieth year after the foundation of Rome; there is no doubt that the Lamb of God is being crucified each day, and will be until the end of the world. Yet it is as if now the crucifixion has at last become fully a historical reality. It is in our day that Jesus is, in the fullest and most radical sense, being rejected by everything—I mean literally everything— and in every area of man's endeavors: his thinking, his willing, his undertakings, his building of his world, his consumption, etc. It is in our day that Jesus is being, in the fullest and most radical sense, humiliated: simply left aside as possessing no interest or significance in comparison with what man discovers for himself and bestows upon himself. It is in our day that Jesus is, in the fullest and most radical sense, being put to death, since none of his words or actions or miracles have any relevance for Eros-inspired man.

As long as the crucifixion of Jesus was the focus of men's interests and eyes and thoughts, he was not truly crucified. In our day, the means man has acquired have made him turn his eyes and thoughts and consciousness away from the cross; the cross is good for nothing now but to mark men's graves. Now Jesus has truly been crucified, in the fullest sense that the word "crucifixion" can have as the sign and symbol of scorn, derision, unimportance, failure, abandonment. But think what this entails. It means that God has been conquered and eliminated from the society to which he once issued his challenge. The cross of Jesus, which was meant to be the sign of God's unconquerable love, has now become purely and simply the sign of his failure. Eros has triumphed through technical and political advances.[34] God has fallen silent.

The silence is the great silence that the evangelists tell us descended at the moment of the crucifixion and which had such tragic meaning for Jesus. It is the great silence that the Apocalypse tells us fell upon creation as the Lamb broke open the seventh seal. It is the silence of God, who is Word yet has now withdrawn into speechlessness. The God of the Word no longer reveals himself, no longer makes himself heard. We cannot say that the noise of the world and the words exalted by the mass-communications media have drowned out the Word of God. No, it is simply that God no longer speaks.

Here, it seems to me, we have a new challenge issued by God to this world. The man of the modern age wanted to slay the Father; now, by eliminating the Son as he has, he has in effect slain the Father. He wanted to substitute his own power for the supposed or revealed power of God. He has worked miracles which seem divine (like the Pharaoh's magicians, who were as powerful as Moses and worked the same miracles as he did: the whole hermeneutical problem was already posed at that moment). He has mastered creation and has no further need of providence. He sees within his grasp the fulfillment of the age-old dreams he used to tell God about in his prayers. He knows there is no more need of forgiveness for sin, because sin is just a sickness. He need not look to God for truth, because he has taken the path of "research and development," and this path will lead him to all the answers. Salvation is no longer from the Jews or from God; man saves himself through his sciences and his technical skill.

Indeed, we may ask, what could God still have to say to man? What could he possibly still mean to man? The God who was once revealed in his self-humiliation is still being revealed in his present humiliation, and only in this humiliation! It is nothing but a monstrous show of human pride to extend the humiliation that God deliberately accepted and experienced in Jesus, to all suffering, unfortunate, humiliated, and exploited human beings. The theologians who assert that only in the persons of the poor do we encounter Jesus and that the poor alone are God's image (the famous "horizontal relationship") are simply theologians of Eros and human pride. They are inspired by the spirit of the world and are contributing to the accomplishment of man's purpose, which is to strip God of his work and his very identity, to strip him of what he chose to be.

These theologians are today's chief priests and members of the Sanhedrin who rend their garments at the scandal of Jesus declaring himself God. They are today's Pharisees, far more so than the priests and pastors of another day with their attachments to institutions, who are now lost in the shadows of a history that is over and done with. By thus stripping God in the realm of theology, these theologians are finishing the work western man has done in other areas. And by so doing, they are effectively humiliating God and crucifying Jesus. Like Jesus before Pilate, God remains silent in the face of the insulting accusation; in what may well be the final combat, God remains silent.

God's silence means that the world that wanted to be left alone is now indeed alone. It is left to its own dereliction. In writing those words, I am not proposing a hypothesis or a personal interpretation. I am simply repeating what the entire Bible tells us, namely, that God adapts himself to man, walks with man along the paths man chooses, and enters into a relationship with man in which God is the Wholly Other and yet is also inexpressibly close to man.

God's silence also means that an event has occurred that is of capital importance for the history of the West. If, as I have tried to show, the history of the West is constituted by the tension and conflict between Eros and Agape, between man's ambition to be completely dominant and the humility of God among us; if this history is the ever renewed result of the reciprocal challenges of man and God; if the meaning of man's undertakings springs precisely from this relationship that was established by the Word of God: then the silence of God entails the disappearance of the very meaning of western history; that history is now annulled and rendered impossible. The paradox that is the West exists no longer.

From now on, all that is left is a drab, insipid unfolding of implications, an interplay of forces and mechanisms. There will be structures and systems, but we shall no longer be able to speak of "history." Man is now seeing the very purpose of his struggling being removed from him, as well as every opportunity for a more intense life; he may continue to "fight," but his fists will encounter only empty air and unbounded darkness. God's absence means the abandonment of the world, but in this world man will discover that he himself is likewise absent. When the West claims a monopoly of the truth and seeks to proclaim it to others, it will arouse only anger and hatred. The West is dying because it has won out over God.[35]

CHAPTER II

THE TRULY POOR AND THE END OF THE LEFT

The Left has traveled the same road that the West in its entirety had traveled before it. All that gave reality and substance to the West had ended in an impasse. The Christianity that had sustained the West for so many centuries ended in tyranny, the negation of its own values, ecclesiastical oppression, and the exploitation of the poor. History was a bloodstream in which the blood had congealed. Then came the short interlude of liberal, bourgeois, capitalist democracy. The latter still asserted the values the West had discovered, and exalted the individual, reason, and freedom, but the values it proclaimed were abstractions; they were algebraic signs and hypocritical justifications of a reality that was utterly different.

This was the impasse into which the Left talked itself, the swamp into which it plunged. The anarchist Left took the individual and freedom with complete and radical seriousness. It made no concessions, but played a tragic game of double or nothing. The socialist Left was more prudent in its approach; it might speak of the dictatorship of the proletariat, or of communism, or of socialism, but, in Marx at least, the end in view was always the individual and his freedom. The goal of the great adventure Marx describes is not at all the loss of individuality proper to a termite nest, but, on the contrary, the development of man's specific individuality (which has nothing to do with nineteenth-century individualism) and the true experience of freedom.

The entire Left was at one in proclaiming the triumph of reason and requiring clarity from an intellect that had now been rescued from the obscurantism of religion. The Left based its whole program on the supposition that language and communication were possible. It took up the reins of history where Christianity had dropped them, and set out on the same road to exalt the same values that Christianity had. At the same time, moreover, as it made its own the discovery of history, the Left also made its own the discovery of revolution. Thus the whole of the West was in the hands of the Left. The Left was now the bearer of all western values, and it seemed that a new age was opening up before us.

In 1930 all our hopes were centered on the Left. What did the Right mean to us—the Right that claimed to represent the tradition of the West but in fact had completely falsified that tradition? Neither Thiers nor Maurras represented anything that was true about the West.[1] We saw only too clearly what the Right, in any of its forms from capitalism to fascism, really represented: the diametrical opposite of all the great values the West had discovered, the shadow side and the cruelty that had marked western history, the wretchedness and the lies that had accompanied that history. The Left alone, with its great and generous vision, its gaze turned toward the future, and its determination to advance ever further, truly embodied the West that had been forged in the fires of the last two thousand years.

The Left, and only the Left, made its own all the values proper to the West, while also breaking new paths. The Left was in the process of adding something new to this amazing history. We saw earlier how the West had discovered within itself the bad conscience, that habit of reflecting on itself and challenging itself. The Left was so deeply struck with this aspect of western history that it focused its attention on the main accusation the West could level against itself: the existence of its poor.

The Left proclaimed the rights of the poor, it was determined to defend them, it turned them into the standard bearers of the future. The Left paved the way for justice to the poor. Undoubtedly, the West had in the past frequently endeavored to do justice to the poor by successive additions to its laws (the manner of doing so had differed in Greece, at Rome, and in Christianity), but social justice had never become a reality. Social justice had been felt as a possibility but never experienced; it had been prophesied but never realized; it had never been given its proper content and its full dimensions that embraced society as a whole.

Without losing anything of its own proper character, the Left laid hold of the idea of social justice and was determined to make it a reality. By so doing, the Left entered fully into the ongoing stream of western development. In this process, each new wave incorporated the movement and acquisitions of the preceding wave, and proceeded to develop the virtualities already present. The Left was now endeavoring to bring to fruition the intuitions of Greece and the promises of Christianity.

But the Left was bent on doing a good deal more than that, for, in undertaking the defense of the poor, it was also endeavoring to repair the harm done by the West. The triumphal advance of the West and its expansion in every area had exacted a heavy price in the form of increased poverty. The West had built on blood, destruction, and suffering; it had left in its wake the proletariat, the subproletariat, peoples colonized, robbed, uprooted, urbanized, starved, and enslaved. The time had come for the West to heed its own bad conscience, fix its eyes on its own true values, and attempt to repair, heal, and win forgiveness. The Left undertook this absolutely necessary task and in the process was to carry the West to heights no other civilization had ever reached.

But who, in fact, were "the poor"? The question is an apparently simple one, but it proved to be a rock on which the whole venture would suffer shipwreck.

1 The Truly Poor

We said earlier that the West, by its very existence, by its mere presence, had led to the division, first, of its own society, then of the entire world, into rich and poor. Rich and poor had always existed, but this juxtaposition did not turn into an opposition, a division, a conflict between men until the West came on the scene. As we have developed, however, the concept of poverty has changed.

There was a time when the rich person was the one who possessed money and could spend it (buy what he pleased) and live in luxury. I deliberately speak of "money," since land was not at that time thought of chiefly as wealth and as the basis for economic relations; land was first and foremost the base of political power. The rich man was chiefly the man who engaged in trade, and consequently the very idea of wealth was essentially associated with cities. If a man possessed land, he was in a position to command; he had power over men and could exercise justice over the inhabitants of his domain; he could raise an army from among them to fight against his neighbors or defend himself against their incursions. Such a person could at the same time be quite poor. Agriculture was carried on, and rentals came in to the owner, but, despite what the Marxist myth says, all this was not regarded as the most important thing.

The lord of the manor, then, was not necessarily rich, and the rich man did not necessarily become lord of a manor. Wealth and land were two forms of power representing different scales of value, and they could not be assimilated, any more than economic power and political power can be assimilated or even confused. The opposition of which we are here speaking between rich and poor had existed prior to the period of the bourgeoisie in the West, but when it did appear, it was essentially a European phenomenon of the period when the characteristic traits of the western world came to life and bulked large. (We have already observed that in certain periods of western civilization—for example, from the fifth to the twelfth centuries—these characteristics vanished, as it were, and society fell into a sleep in which the traditional, archetypal dreams of mankind came to life once again.)

For almost three centuries now, we have been seeing a new direction taken in the matter of wealth. It is this: everything is changed into an economic value, into wealth or a source of wealth. The earth and every human activity are assigned an economic value, and this value is given priority and becomes the measure of everything. Even the political has been affected by this trend, although it has not yielded completely. Political power that is relatively independent of economic power continues to exist, especially as the world has become a smaller place in which all peoples are related each to the others and in which political power may result not from the intrinsic importance of a state and its people nor from its wealth but, for example, from its geographical location, which may give it considerable value in the eyes of the other powers. There is no question in such cases of possible natural resources that might be exploited by the great powers. (Tiny Panama is very important politically, as is Cuba.)

A nation may also lack intrinsic power, yet be powerful because of its relationship to one or other powerful nation, the latter being, in our day, a rich nation. Thus economic wealth (not monetary wealth) is the basis of political power for some nations (and the converse is also true), but for the majority the fact of being allied with a rich and powerful nation is the basis of their existence and ultimately of their wealth. Here, the nation in question may have no intrinsic wealth; its wealth is its alliance with the wealthy and powerful.

There is a third, likewise new, aspect to wealth in our age. In a technically oriented society, the fact of owning capital or being able to convert resources into capital is regarded as less important than the possession of talented individuals, diplomas, and the ability to exercise functions that are much in demand. Such intellectual capacity (or possibly even ability that is purely technical in character) makes a nation rich today.

This leads in turn to a fourth aspect of wealth in our age. A person is rich today who has access to sources of information and is able, should the occasion arise, to use the information media for the purpose of broadcasting himself or spreading news or swaying public opinion or simply making himself known to others. What this last amounts to is a rather strange return to the idea of "fame" that was so important in antiquity. It may be that fame or celebrity, that is, the good opinion people have of you (this presupposes, of course, that you are sufficiently well known to "people"), was as important in China, India, and Africa, as it was in the western world. Perhaps, but I do not think it was.

In any case, even among the Jews "fame" was regarded as essential. That is, a man had to have a name in the eyes of other people; that name had to be known to as many other individuals as possible; mention of the name had to call up positive images, and the memory of the person had to stir others to praise of him. All that was very important. In Egypt we see the Pharaoh similarly anxious to be known and appreciated. The difference between Egypt and Israel was that in Egypt such worries afflicted only the ruler, while in Israel everyone was concerned about fame or a good name.

We find this very same concern later on in democratic Greece, then in republican and imperial Rome. The idea of fame (which, in the sixteenth century, will become again, as in Egypt, chiefly a concern for the glory of the king) will constantly gain ground thereafter; men regard the judgment others pass on them as extremely important. Frequently a good name will be set in the scales against riches: "A good reputation is more valuable than money."[2] The bourgeoisie will be especially concerned about a good name: no one must be able to say anything bad about you. The reason for this concern in the bourgeoisie is the close connection between economic activity and the confidence of the public; a man cannot succeed in business if his reputation is not above reproach. That is why the failure in business has no out but suicide; he has no future in anything requiring economic activity. Moreover, it is not enough to have a good name among a small circle of friends; your reputation must be good with customers, suppliers, competitors, etc.

Reputation becomes all the more important as your circle of acquaintances grows. The twentieth century has witnessed a very remarkable change in this area. It can be said that until the twentieth century reputation was a matter of "moral" value; that is, reputation was a matter of the judgments people passed on a person's moral conduct, and this, almost inevitably, in a rather limited circle of acquaintances. In that earlier time, a reputation that could be justly called "fame" required some action out of the ordinary. The individual had to have had an outstanding career or have become a hero. Once he did, however, the evaluation of him lost its moral component; there was no longer any concern with the moral quality of his action, and all attention was focused on the action or career that won him "glory." That kind of glory was regarded as not subject to the judgments that might be passed on the ordinary man. The larger the number of people a man's fame reached, the less that fame seemed subject to any moral evaluation. Great fame took a man outside the realm of moral values. It is clear, however, that before the twentieth century only a small number of individuals could acquire such widespread fame.

The change, to which we referred above as having taken place in this century, has been due to the extension of the communications media. Nowadays a vast number of hearers, readers, or spectators can be made aware of a large number of facts and personalities. Since, moreover, the media must constantly be fed, there is need of a continual supply of heroes and stars.[3] Some of these heroes and stars stay around for a long time, but few for very long. John F. Kennedy was forgotten in a few months. After dominating the public scene, Kennedy, Khrushchev, and Pope John XXIII quickly vanished from the scene, and people soon discovered how wrong they had been to regard these men as so able and to believe that they would change the world. The same holds true for the actors, singers, and scholars who suddenly move into the spotlight; they soon disappear, as Lévi-Strauss has into the dark night of academe.

This widespread fame of a very large number of individuals

has the same characteristics as traditional fame and glory. First of all, it has no connection with moral value and ethical behavior. A person who is judged adversely by his immediate entourage, which knows him well, may have achieved through the media a universal reputation that is just the opposite. Gisèle Halimi might pay her housekeeper half the salary set by law, but that is unimportant, since no one knows about it; everyone knows, however, that she is a Joan of Arc waging war in behalf of women, the poor, and the oppressed: a real saint![4]

Moral values reappear on the scene only as a weapon when a group sets out to use the media to ruin the reputation of an enemy. The Watergate affair is a prime example. Richard Nixon did what every head of state does today, and everyone knew this. Yet the conscience of the world was suddenly roused when, in a carefully planned scheme, a group of Nixon's enemies denounced, in the name of a moral code no one believes in any more, Nixon's extraordinary, frightful machinations. Once public attention was caught, the man was done for.

Fame, however, does not depend on morality. When a person's moral character is emphasized in order to enhance his reputation, this tactic has but one purpose: the good conscience and self-justification of the group that calls the public's attention to the man's moral stature. The Abbé Pierre was celebrated for his virtue because such a reputation helped French society prove it was interested in authentic values.[5] The same thing holds for Jean-Paul Sartre, of course, and for the Russell War Crimes Tribunal. Morality has no place in the media unless it is of use to the public.

The second way in which the widespread fame of individuals today resembles traditional fame and glory is that it is a form of wealth. An individual may be poor himself, but if he wins celebrity through the media, he is necessarily counted among the rich. You may be a poor person in your private life, but if public opinion is on your side, if the eye of the television camera is on you, or if your voice is heard on the radio, you are richer (richer, not just more powerful!) than if you had a portfolio of investments. The two kinds of wealth often go together, and, thanks to the media, money may start pouring in.

It remains true, however, that simply to be known and recognized by others—not by a few neighbors but by the millions of television viewers—is a form of wealth. The sick person with the strange illness who wins the interest of a nation because they have spoken of him on the radio, is no longer the same sick person he was before. He can now die in peace, for he is more famous that Louis XIV ever was (not for as long, of course; but, after all, in our century the moment is the important thing). The man who suffered greatly in a concentration camp and then later on lost his whole family in an accident can survive and build himself a new personality when, though he has nothing but troubles to tell, he tells them in a way that makes him famous. The hundreds of thousands of readers and the millions of television viewers who weep as they learn of his sufferings form a human retinue that makes up for the ancient consolations afforded by belief in God. The man has become rich by winning public attention through the mass communications media.

This analysis of the factors that constitute wealth and of their development is indispensable if we are to understand, by contrast, what poverty means in our world. The poverty people automatically think of is, of course, economic poverty. The poor man is the one whose salary has been cut, who is exploited, who has only the bare minimum needed to sustain life, and who is not a consumer of the good things of our society; he is the person who does not share in "the ownership of the means of production." There is your poor man! If we turn to groups, the poor are those who hold the menial jobs which others regard with contempt (thus the immigrant groups in the West) and the peoples of the third world who are dominated and exploited and who die of hunger. This is the first and most obvious meaning we give to "poverty."

We must also, however, consider the poverty that relates to power and means; I shall speak of this as political poverty. I am referring to those who lack the means of intervening with the authorities, those who lack influence, those whom the administration thinks of as the "vulgar herd," the people who do not share in any decision-making and on whom the laws are simply imposed. I am referring to those whose only weapon is the laughable one of the ballot they cast from time to time, and who are deprived even of this since they must follow a political party if they want their "voice" to count; if they do not line up with a party, their "voice" is useless, lost, the more so as they express a more reflective and noteworthy view of their own.

The man who is politically poor has no choice but to lose himself completely in the anonymity of the crowd if he wants his vote to have any chance of changing anything. Only two courses are open to him. His voice can remain his own, expressing his real sufferings, his own experience, his personal passion, but then it will not be heard; it will be useless, lost. Or he may lend his voice to a mass organization that is made up precisely of many abandoned voices; then a change can be effected, but the voice of the person who contributed to form the crowd is lost (as an individual reality) just as much as before.

Political poverty may be located at the meeting point of economic poverty and poverty in regard of fame. For about twenty years now we have been seeing the proletariat making the important claim that they should be able to share in decision-making. In other words, the workers now want not only better salaries; they also want somehow to share in the decisions made by the authorities, the administrative decisions that are translated into orders and commands. When a man does nothing but carry out decisions imposed on him, he is stripped of a part of his personhood, even if his salary enables him to live fairly well. He is still a poor man.

The same concept of poverty is applicable to nations. The poor nations are the ones that have no means of sharing in decisions that concern them. The whole world became aware of this aspect of the real situation at the time of the 1973 war between Israel and Egypt. Peace was imposed on the two countries when Russia and the United States got together and came to an agreement over the heads of both parties. No account was taken either of Israel or of Egypt. Israel could not pursue its offensive drive after the first victory because the United States vetoed it. The Arabs, despite their conviction that they could still save the day, and their will to do so, could not act because Russia, too, had imposed a veto. The United States and Russia were engaged in a chess game in which the two fighting nations were pawns. At that moment both Israel and Egypt were poor nations; they were poor because they lacked the technology that would have enabled them to make autonomous political decisions.

This kind of poverty can be offset by alliances with powerful nations. We cannot rightly say that nations which are really supported by (and to that same degree subject to) one of the three great powers are really poor. They are lieges of one or other of the three great lords of war, but this allegiance brings them real political (and military) power. The only condition is that they surrender their autonomy; they thus reflect, at the international level, the situation already described of voters and their "voice."

There is a third kind of poverty: poverty with regard to fame and reputation. In this case, the poor man is the one who is forgotten, the one whom nobody knows and recognizes. We pointed out above that the lack of participation in decision-making is related to this kind of poverty. The person who does not participate is not recognized by others for his ability or his dignity or his very existence; he is simply an object and an instrument. Lack of recognition leads to lack of reputation. The broadcasting of a name to the world brings a kind of wealth; forgetfulness plunges a man into nothingness; the combatants who are forgotten are twice dead.[6]

Authoritarian regimes know perfectly well what they are doing, then, when they rewrite history so that the name of an enemy or a hero, a Trotsky or a Confucius, disappears from its pages. As long as a man's memory survives, he remains, though dead, rich and potentially dangerous. In our own time, anyone who does not have public opinion behind him is a poor man, and indeed terribly deprived. The reason is that nowadays, thanks to the communications media, every event becomes a world affair. Everything concerns everyone, and in the last analysis the individual is rich because he is supported by everyone else. In this astounding concert of exchanges, however, in which we see the Chilean guerrillas supported by meetings in Greece, and the Greek guerrillas supported by meetings in Paris, and so on, the person of whom no one says anything is truly the most abandoned of men.

Such was evidently not the case in the days when the affairs of the individual, even his political affairs, were of interest only to a small group who constituted his immediate entourage. But how is it possible today not to feel deeply frustrated when we see public opinion, the press, and television converging, finding fault, accusing, and encouraging the participants in this or that international drama, while we know that we our-selves are involved in the same kind of situation, but no one is interested! In this whole business of poverty, reputation or, in current terms, support or condemnation by public opinion, is the decisive thing, even though the public opinion is created by the media. This kind of poverty is much more important than we may be inclined to think. In fact, it is probably the most important kind of all today, as we shall try to show.

Thus, we have three kinds of, or aspects of, poverty, and they go together. There are those who die of hunger, and no one speaks of them; there are those who suffer political op-pression, and no one speaks of them. There are those who suffer political oppression and die of hunger, and no one speaks of them.

We must move on now to a new analysis, since in this matter of wealth and poverty there is another distinction that must be made, namely, the distinction between the individuals who make up a people, and the people in its entirety, the people as a nation or political body. There can, for example, be a political poverty of the entire people and/or of the individuals who make up the people. This division comes from the West, not in the sense that the West is the direct cause of it (the West did not effect the separation of people and individual), but in the sense that it has certainly been the occasion for it.

In speaking of wealth and poverty in regard to fame, we saw

that it was the media, as developed and used by the West, that determined whether a man was to be rich or poor in fame. In a similar manner, it is the western invention of the abstract concept of the nation and national greatness, on the one hand, and, on the other, the western invention of abstract wealth (financial and economic) that make it possible for a social body to be rich while its members are poor; another factor has been the entirely theoretical and (as is increasingly admitted) erroneous idea of the gross national product.

Traditionally, the (economic) wealth of a group was the sum-total of the wealth of its members. The group's political power was the sum-total of the military effectiveness of each member. This is no longer the case. A nation may now be very rich while its members are very poor; the Arab peoples provide a typical example. Conversely, nations may be very poor (politically, for example), though its members are individually rich and no one pities them. An example would be the Scandinavian countries which are practically nonexistent as political powers or even as economic powers. How often do we think of this side of the coin?

If we want to see who in our world has power and who is poor, we must combine the distinction of nation and individual with our earlier three types of wealth and poverty (economic; political; wealth and poverty in terms of fame). You hear people saying with a catch in their throats that the Arabs are the real poor of our times. It is true enough that individual Arabs are dreadfully poor in Egypt, Arabia, Yemen; that they are constantly undernourished; that they do not develop. On the other hand, the Arab peoples cease to be poor by the very fact that world opinion proclaims them to be poor! Everyone talks about the Arab peoples and is concerned about them. Next, they are powerful and rich as nations. They form a group that can speak out as loudly and forcefully as the three great powers because they have the oil the world needs. The Arab nations are rich, not poor. If you want to see how stupid the talk of the gross national product is, just be bold enough to calculate the gross national product of Saudi Arabia in terms of the income from oil, and you will see that the average income is a good deal higher than it is for the United States.

We are confronted, then, with a fearful gap between the daily reality of individual lives and the greatness of the nation on the international scene. "But that is due to the capitalist structure of the countries in question" (i.e., the Arab countries). Things are not that simple. To begin with, the capitalism in these countries is a feudal capitalism. Second, and more important, the Arabs lack an overall psychological adaptation to the way political power must be exercised in our world.

Some Arabs are not only feudal lords without any interest in the welfare of their people; they are extremely limited as men of state, and are incapable of properly managing a nation, its wealth, or a war. The poverty of the Arab peoples is due above all to the incompetence of their leaders. In order to make this clear, I must say a few words about Arabian petroleum politics.

One of the most interesting things about the last few months[7] is that, despite the flood of articles on the "oil crisis," there has been almost complete silence when it comes to evaluating the Arab governments and their political maturity. (I say "Arab governments," not "Arab peoples," for the peoples do not have, and never have had, anything to say about it in Algeria or Saudi Arabia or any other Arab country.) Some journalists, as we might expect, have waxed enthusiastic about the fact that the Arabs at last had a tool that gave them political power; that they were now bringing the western giant to its knees; that they could at last follow an independent policy of their own.

In the following paragraphs I am not trying to defend the West (all the less since I am convinced that the oil crisis is not as serious as all that). Still less am I trying to defend technological progress. I am far from deploring the fact that the West has been brought up short; on the contrary, I rejoice that the politics based on technical energy power has perhaps been forced to slow down somewhat. For myself, I would feel a deep satisfaction if someday we were to be without automobiles entirely. The point here, however, has nothing to do with our future but with the unparalleled superficiality the Arab governments have shown in their handling of this whole business.

The Arabs have (and have long had) the means of holding their own against the West and even of blackmailing the West, but they have now been using it in the most stupid way possible. They have not manifested the least bit of political intelligence, but have reacted like a youngster who has a hand grenade and throws it simply because he is impatient, irritable, and tired, without calculating the effects at all. I shall not dwell on the startling swings shown in the successive decisions the Arabs have taken. It seems to me, however, that we can draw three conclusions from the action of the Arab governments in the oil embargo and the raising of prices for the product.

First, then, the Arab governments have clearly acted on the spur of the moment and without at all asking themselves what would happen. They have had only one purpose: to punish the peoples who support Israel. Could any approach to politics be more frighteningly simplistic than that? "Ah, but they are also interested, in part, in destroying the West." Perhaps, but, as well as piling up money, they have been trying to buy, from that same West, fully equipped factories and all the other things they need in order to become themselves an industrial nation! In other words, their very wealth will either be useless or will contribute to the industrial prosperity of Europe and America, which for the time being must continue to depend on oil.

At the same time, the Arab governments are adversely affecting Russia, their ally and support, so much so that Russia will have to stop supplying oil to its satellites. This means that the European countries that will really be hurt are Bulgaria, Hungary, Czechoslovakia, and Poland. In addition, economists are agreed that the oil crisis can only strengthen the superpowers economically and technically. That is to say that in the five years ahead Russia and the United States will profit by this difficult situation. There is an example of clever politics for you! Conversely, the countries that will suffer most from the Arab decisions are India and the African countries—not Germany and England. For India, the situation is really tragic. So, stop the nonsense about the solidarity of the third-world nations and the imperialist exploitation of those countries; in the present crisis the Arabs are acting just like any other imperialist. Of course, the Hindus are nothing but contemptible Buddhists, and the Arab Muslims would be quite content to strangle them all. In short, everything proves that what the Arab world is confronting us with is irresponsible and poorly thought-out political decisions.

The second conclusion we draw from what has been happening is this: the Arab governments have shown themselves incapable of controlling their own power in an orderly way. They have become intoxicated by the spectacle they are providing; their attitude is, "Just watch our next move!" This suggests two reflections. First, if the Arab governments possessed other forms of power, they would use them in the same spontaneous, incautious way. What does that tell us about the Arabs and the atom bomb? Give the bomb to Colonel Qaddafi, and he would destroy the world in the next six months. No "balance of terror" would stop one of the Arab potentates if he took it into his head to see the big bomb go off.

Second, there is Israel. The Arabs have shown themselves incapable of properly handling their own victory (a victory in the oil market, not on the battlefield); they want to press their advantage ruthlessly and to the utmost. Can we imagine them acting any differently if they did conquer Israel? No; the oil crisis shows that when the Arabs are on top, they do not know when to stop. Thus, if ever they gained the upper hand over Israel, they would be satisfied with nothing but the total extermination of its people. They would show no more moderation (less, if anything) in a victorious military war than they have been showing in the oil war. The oil crisis has given us clear evidence that the Arabs lack maturity, moderation, self-control. I am sure that if the Arabs had been about to conquer when the last war with Israel ended, they would not have obeyed the United Nations order for a cease-fire. The Israelis were winning, but they obeyed the order. The Arabs have shown their lack of self-control when they are victorious. They want no limitations; at present, for example, they want to gain an incalculable financial power, even though, as has been

shown, there comes a point when such power becomes meaningless. No matter to the Arabs: they think they are rich because they can add up their billions of dollars.

The third conclusion we draw from Arab behavior in the oil
crisis is that the Arab governments are completely lacking in
political foresight. The technical societies (i.e., the societies
based on rational efficiency) have already begun to draw the
right conclusions from the Arab attitude: the Arabs have fool-
ishly been thinking of oil as the only practical source of energy,
the cheapest source; they have been putting all their eggs in
one basket. Consequently, the technicians of the western
world have set about solving the great problem of the moment: "What can we use to replace oil at every level (and not
just for energy)?" We need not worry: in five years the inven-
tive western world will have found the way—many ways—to
replace oil as a source of energy and to provide substitutes for
the industrial byproducts of petroleum. But won't that require
an economic reconversion? Of course it will. But it will not be
the first (or the last); in 1945, after the Second World War, the
United States managed just as difficult a reconversion.

The Arabs have taught the West a lesson, and the West has
learned it: do not rely on a single source of energy; do not rely
on the Arabs. The West will change its ways, and in five years
"the Arabs can go and gargle with their oil," as I heard a
worker on the subway train put it. The Arabs have shown their
political immaturity by throwing away their future for the sake
of an immediate spectacular success. They have not taken to
heart Machiavelli's principle that you should not unleash your
entire power against an enemy so long as you are not sure you
can eliminate him for good. The Arabs, as a result, have lost
not only their war against Israel; they have already lost their
oil war as well. You cannot properly say that the Arabs are the
poorest of the poor. Their power is terrifying—but absurd!

In writing as I have, I am not taking a position against the
Arab countries; I am simply pointing out their lack of maturity
and strict self-control. As a matter of fact, I am grieved at the
mistakes they have made. I will go even further and say that
I do not believe there is really an oil crisis. For one thing, the

price increases that seem so enormous to us simply mean that the price of oil is catching up. For the last twenty years, the price of oil has in fact gone down by comparison with other living costs. We have lived under the politics of cheap energy, but the cheapness meant we were robbing the countries that produced the oil. The sudden rise in price only brought the price of oil into parity with other prices as of 1958.

Where is the crisis, then? If we could have lived with such oil prices in 1958, why can we not do it in 1974? The only reason would be that we have meanwhile built a production system that depends on exploitation of the oil countries. It seems to me, however, that one cause of western greatness is the ability of the West to acknowledge its own faults. If a fault is really a fault, we must repent of it.

A further point we perhaps ought to emphasize in this whole business is that we have all the noise and drama and propaganda because the people "at fault" are the Arabs. By this I mean that if it were the United States that had taken such decisions, people would have reacted much more calmly and would not have emphasized the difficulties the capitalist countries are facing (the Left would, of course). The incredible noise and fury that has accompanied OPEC and its decisions for the past year has sprung solely from the desire of western capitalism to level charges at the Arab countries.[8]

In describing the opposition between individual wealth and national wealth, we must give an important place to the gagged peoples who live under terrorist regimes. In a very large number of cases, terror has become the surest means of holding on to collective power. Here we must remind ourselves of something I have said on other occasions (as have many other writers): year by year the "liberal" or "democratic" regimes, which, though far from satisfactory, do not seek the political power of the nation at the expense of the political power of individuals, are vanishing and being replaced by threatening modern nations that are drunk on national greatness. The democracies are becoming fewer on the world map.

The communist countries, of course, base their power on the strict enslavement of all the citizenry; there is no need to go into all that again. Meanwhile, the military dictatorships are growing more numerous each year, from Brazil to Uganda, from Burma to Chile. The peoples who are thus gagged, controlled, and held in submission by police dictatorships are poor peoples indeed. Yet the nations they form are growing greater and asserting themselves economically and politically. Nowadays, it seems, we must regard these two statements as necessarily connected. That is, it seems that in the seventies of this century a state can become powerful and rich only by enslaving the individual citizens.

What has happened in the socialist states is no accident. There is only an apparent opposition between the slavery of the concentration camps and the growth of the police and the propaganda, on the one hand, and, on the other, the industrialization, the acquisition of international authority, and national greatness and wealth. The first set of phenomena is in fact a direct condition of the second; the first is inevitable if the second is to be attained. The same thing will happen in the third-world countries that are entering the competition. It has already happened in China (to the great scandal, I am sure, of those who admire the happy contentment of the Chinese), which by no means presents us with a "new model of development."

Collective greatness comes only at the price of individual bloodshed and unhappiness. There is no other way. The splendid ideology of harmonious growth in which the general interest would be simply the sum-total of the prosperities of individuals, and the interests of individuals would converge to produce collective development, is nothing but an idyll. We can predict with certainty that all the peoples whose states are now committed to development are unhappy peoples, and that their unhappiness will intensify as development becomes more rapid. Sadly enough, the West had already shown the way in this respect, for the West had already made the proletarian class more wretched than it had been before, and it was on the incredible suffering of this class that the grand and glorious "technological society" was built. The glory was so great that other countries can now think of nothing but imitating the West; they forget the price that was paid, and lull themselves with the dream that this kind of power can be acquired without paying for it.

Among the countries showing this basic discrepancy between collective greatness and individual wretchedness, I must give North Vietnam a special place, even if it means shocking my readers. We have all read the countless articles on the incredible heroism of the people of Vietnam who, though overwhelmed by bombs, retained their cohesiveness and carried on the war. And how often we have heard the war between Vietnam and the United States compared to the combat of David with Goliath! How often it has been said that this tiny country checkmated the greatest military power of the age—a proof, surely, of the excellence of the Vietnamese regime and the heroism of the North Vietnamese people who were roused by patriotic feeling and were unanimous in the struggle!

That picture needs considerable modification. To begin with, let us recall the simple fact that there was no confrontation between the United States and Vietnam. The United States did bombard the country, blockade the ports, and so on, but everyone knows that only the invasion of an enemy's territory can bring a war to an end. No bombing has ever made a people surrender. (The bomb that fell on Hiroshima did, of course, but it is crystal-clear that if the United States had obliterated Hanoi with a hydrogen bomb, Vietnam would have surrendered like Japan.) The German people were crushed by bombardments for two years, but they were not at all ready to surrender in 1944; it took another year of fighting and the invasion of German territory by armies ten times more powerful than the German army to bring about the capitulation. The same would have been true of North Vietnam: if it had been invaded, it would have surrendered. China made such an invasion impossible.

Vietnam, then, was not a poor isolated little country facing a colossus; the colossus could not set foot in Vietnamese territory because another colossus stood ready to interfere and protect Vietnam. The Vietnamese themselves were certainly unhappy, poor, wretched, and terrorized, but the State of Vietnam had a mighty protector, and this made her as powerful as the United States.

Let us advance a bit further into this forbidden area. The Vietnamese held up amazingly amid so much suffering, but they did so in the way the Germans did under Nazism. They held out because the North Vietnamese regime is a ruthless dictatorship. We should never forget the massacres and deportations that accompanied the establishment of good old Papa Ho's regime; they were worthy of a Hitler or a Stalin. In addition, a constant indoctrination, strict regulation, police system, and ruthless repression forced this unhappy people to be silent and heroically obedient. There was no way to escape.

I marvel at the French and American intellectuals who, sharing as they do the Vietnamese regime's views, are invited by the government to visit the country, and who manage to "see everything" in three weeks. They bring back with them a vision of perfect, idyllic joy among the people and of their high cultural level; the visitors can attest the absence of internment camps and of any system of repression. In the same way, Henri Béraud could swear that there were absolutely no concentration camps in Germany; Madame Joliot-Curie could say the same for Russia, and that fine woman Simone de Beauvoir for Cuba (unfortunately, Castro himself said only a few months later that camps did exist for reeducation through work).[9] All this is part of western man's amazing blindness. When these scholars and intellectuals become committed partisans, they are more stupid (in the etymological sense of "benumbed") than a bird held spellbound by a snake. They see nothing. They abandon the critical approach. They are incapable of controlling what people tell them. They believe. And the more absurd the things they are told, the more they believe. *Credo quia absurdum:* I believe because it is absurd.

This well-known theological commonplace has today become a political commonplace. We have a recent and quite wonderful example of it in a series of articles written for *Le Monde* by François Wahl.[10] Wahl is an able philosopher and a virtuoso in handling ideas, yet, after three weeks in China, he makes a number of astounding statements. He tells us that in China there is no apparatus for repression, no concentration camps, no economic inequality; that "for the first time" the Chinese have a satisfactory diet; that to achieve the same economic success as the Chinese a capitalist regime would have taken three times as long; that there is no bureaucracy in China; and so forth.

How can a serious-minded intellectual make statements like these after a guided tour of only *three weeks,* during which the hosts were always at his side? Especially in a vast country like China! Did he see Sinkiang? Does he know how difficult it is to spot a bureaucracy? As far as information goes, Wahl's articles are absolutely worthless. This is all the more remarkable since the articles become quite interesting when they turn to theory and the discussion of ideas. When he criticizes ideas and ideological systems, Wahl has a sharp eye for inconsistencies and errors. At this level, which is the level on which he is at home, he has brought out the problem of China quite clearly. But he could have done this just as well without ever leaving his desk in Paris. When it comes to facts and structures, however, his articles are useless, as I said a moment ago. He does not know the facts. Perhaps to his philosopher's mind facts are not worth very much. Perhaps, in his desire to get on with the theory, he found it more convenient to sidestep any discussion of sociological and economic facts. For myself, however, all the subtle theologico-theoretical constructions collapse like a house of cards when confronted by a single concentration camp.

How often must it be repeated that these three-week, or three-month, fact-finding junkets by a few intellectuals become channels for blind propaganda, since the intellectuals who "saw with their own eyes" saw in fact nothing that was really important?

Back to North Vietnam. The Vietnamese people were certainly in wretched straits, doubly so because of the bombing and the regime. But the State of Vietnam was not on that account simply a poor little nation. For one thing, it was under the protection of China, as we noted earlier. For another, we must not forget that Vietnam, made up essentially of what used to be Tonkin, is a nation of warriors. The Tonkinese have been bent on conquest ever since the seventeenth century; they destroyed the Khmer empire and invaded China. We must therefore not misinterpret the present war between North Vietnam and South Vietnam or North Vietnam and Cambodia: these wars are simply the continuation of a process that was interrupted by the French conquest.

The Tonkinese are the invaders; they are just as determined to gain control of all Southeast Asia today as they were a hundred years ago. North Vietnam launched the attack on South Vietnam and began the invasion of Cambodia (well before Lon Nol declared war on it) because it was obeying its historical passion for invasion and conquest. The socialism, the corruption, the injustice in South Vietnam were simply pretexts (we judge these phenomena according to western norms, but North Vietnam does not). The proclamations according to which the Democratic Republic of Vietnam is going to "liberate" other peoples from their oppressive dictators (the oppressive dictators do exist, certainly in South Vietnam, but they are no worse than the dictator in North Vietnam) are nothing but propaganda.

In the same way, the Nazis who invaded France announced quite openly that they were coming to liberate the French from the terrible corruption of democracy and capitalist enslavement, and to bring the rule of justice. In both cases we see a very clever exploitation of sentiments that are indeed abroad in the world, and of one sector of public opinion. These views will, of course, exasperate the good people on the Left who cherish the image of brave little Belgium being invaded in 1914 and see in North Vietnam a pure and holy Joan of Arc: without defects and beyond reproach, yet attacked by ignoble but powerful capitalists who kill for the sake of killing.

The fact is, however, that if the Vietcong had stayed where they were and not attempted to invade South Vietnam, they would never have been attacked. If they had not taken over a thirty-kilometer strip of Cambodian territory, Sihanouk would still be on his throne. Let me say it again: the individual Vietnamese are poor, unhappy victims, but the Vietnamese nation is a powerful conqueror, an invader, an instigator of wars. And its greatest support comes from worldwide public opinion. Here we are faced with a major problem of political poverty.

The nations and governments that are supported by public opinion are among the wealthy, whatever be their other difficulties and problems. World opinion? Does such a thing really exist? We can certainly speak of a division between the views of the Right and the views of the Left, but even this is not a black-and-white distinction. For example, there is no rightist, capitalist, American opinion that is unanimous against an enemy such as Vietnam. At the national level, we can say that there is indeed a single opinion that is given monolithic formulation in the dictatorships, but that there are varied and divergent opinions in the liberal countries.

When we look from abroad at another country, we can grasp the state of opinion in it only through its public expressions. It matters little that millions of Soviet citizens are in secret disagreement with the declarations of their government. They have no way of really expressing themselves (the samizdat, or underground press, is only for intellectuals) and therefore play no role in forming world opinion on a subject. As far as the formation of a world opinion is concerned, there is only the official truth and the expression of it in the newspapers; the latter manifest the preferences of their readers and thus the current of opinion.

A further preliminary point to be made is that the dictatorships of the Right do not concern themselves much with international problems. The Greek, Brazilian, or Chilean newspapers do not speak out extensively in behalf of South Vietnam (the example we have been using) or South Africa or Taiwan. These governments have enough to do handling their internal problems, dealing with the opposition parties, and propagandizing their own people, without getting themselves involved in international problems as well. Consequently, they make no significant contribution to the formation of world opinion.

It is, for practical purposes, the great dictatorships of the

Left, the western democracies, and the third-world countries not run by dictators that form world opinion. We just noted that only monolithic formulations emerge from the dictatorships of the Left. What of the western democracies and the West generally? They seem preoccupied with the defense of capitalist regimes (because they themselves are capitalist) or of the rightist dictatorships (because they themselves are also anticommunist) or of the former colonial powers.

We must distinguish here between fact and opinion. As a matter of fact, the great cartels and the governments of the West can support the various regimes we have just mentioned. But support is not given exclusively to the latter, because business is business, after all, and you sell to anyone who will buy, provided the deal is profitable. Once Mao had won in China, some of the great international capitalists were the first to want recognition of the new regime, because this would pave the way for serious trade with communist China. Clearly, then, these same capitalists will not be blindly and solely in favor of white power in Rhodesia or the Thieu regime in South Vietnam or the Park regime in South Korea.

Matters get much more complicated when we turn to public opinion. Public opinion is, of course, never something spontaneous. The peasant from the mountains of central France, who has never heard of the Thieu regime or of apartheid, will not spontaneously shout himself hoarse demonstrating against them. In fact, even when he does hear of them, it is all the same to him, and he will have no opinions on them. Even if he has opinions garnered from television or newspapers, he is not going to demonstrate. Consequently, he plays no role in the formation of world opinion.

The important role is played by the media themselves and by urban groups that go in for demonstrations. The media function quite differently on the international scene from the way they do on the domestic front. On the domestic front, they are an *agent* in the formation of opinion; this is something I discussed in my book *Propaganda*. At this level, therefore, there is tension and confrontation between the media and opinion. At the international level, however, the media seem to be the *expression* of opinion. I mean that if you want to know what the French are thinking you will read the newspapers and watch the television broadcasts that you regard as representative. At this level, it is through the media that you gain the conviction that a world opinion exists, and through the media that you learn what this opinion is.

You may tell me that in a democracy a wide range of views is represented in the press and that therefore there is no single opinion to be attended to. That is true enough, but only for relatively indifferent matters.

There is another factor that we must now take into account. In the socialist dictatorships, the media are always used as a propaganda tool and serve a tactical purpose. This bit of news, that bit of information: each is geared to obtain a certain effect. It is common knowledge that under dictatorships values and moral judgments play no determining role; they are used simply for their propaganda effect, as arguments for a proposition. In short, dictatorships consciously do what the nineteenth-century bourgeoisie has often been accused of doing unconsciously.

The situation is entirely different in the West. Values and moral judgments may not determine conduct, and principles may be flouted, but the West does believe in certain values, assert a moral code, and depend on principles. "But it only talks about these things; it does not live by them!" We have already seen, however, that this discrepancy is precisely one of the causes of the West's "neurotic personality," since men cannot keep on asserting these values without anything happening. People may not apply the principles, but they do believe in their existence, and the principles and values thus present in people's minds judge the one who disobeys them, and become the cause of bad conscience. In this phenomenon we see the essential wellspring of public opinion in the West.

When Hitler's dictatorial regime revealed itself for what it was, the problem was simple: there was a widespread reaction, and the "free world" found itself unanimous on the solution. This base fellow who flouted all values must be crushed. In this case, self-interest and principles coincided. From 1948 on, however, things became much less clear and simple. How could the West close its ears and heart to the cries for freedom that were emerging from the colonized peoples? The terrible repression in Madagascar left the French people terrified and nauseated. Here, interests conflicted with "feelings," but the feelings were real and gave rise to a bad conscience.

This has been our dilemma ever since. Of course dictatorships are evil; of course racism is evil! We do not want to side with the communists, and, while in the concrete we are racist ourselves, we are so with a bad conscience. The trouble is that neither can we support the anticommunists, because for a half century now communism has been claiming to represent liberty and equality, the very things the French and the Americans supposedly represent. But the communist regimes that have actually arisen by no means exemplify justice and equality. True enough, but everybody knows that this failure is simply an accident of history!

I am not saying that public opinion generally is becoming favorable to the third-world peoples or to communism. It does seem, however, that the western conscience cannot simply reject the value claims these peoples make. The West cannot reject the black's claim to equality with the white, nor his demand for freedom. On the other hand, the West cannot bring itself to give in completely to the claims and the demands, and so it finds itself with an inescapable bad conscience.

Is western opinion, then, divided on these problems? No; as far as its expression is concerned, western opinion is entirely on the side of the third-world peoples and of all who are struggling for equality and justice. As far as its expression is concerned, but not necessarily in its reality. The point is that the values the West proclaims have their existence precisely at the level of expression: they are spoken, proclaimed, affirmed, declared. The proclamation is unchanging; no matter how the West may act, it must keep on speaking the same language. The language in turn formulates public opinion and, at the international level, is taken for the opinion itself.

Public opinion in the West, then, appears and will appear to be on the side of the oppressed peoples and those fighting for their freedom. The West has always claimed to be on the side of David against Goliath, and it continues to make this claim. The difficulty is that the West is now a Goliath, one of the mighty of the earth, yet it cannot but still judge itself according to its old values.

Those most vocal in this whole business are the value-specialists, namely, the intellectuals. There would be no world opinion on South Africa or on the Vietnam war, if it were not for the intellectuals. Does this mean intellectuals are especially honorable men? Not at all! It simply means that this is the only trade they know: they are the specialists in proclaiming values and the manufacturers of moral codes, and they are happy to carry on with their work. Let us note it carefully: intellectuals would cease to exist if they ceased to play this role. This is why Philippe Sollers, who really knows nothing about the matter, thinks himself obliged, as a learned man, to come out in favor of neo-neo-Marxism and China. What else could he do?

In all these questions of values and principles, it is the intellectuals who control the media. Consequently, what the mass media of communication really express (I am speaking of the West, not of the dictatorships) is only the up-to-the-minute majority view of the intellectuals. Intellectuals, however, continue to formulate "the demands of morality" in accordance with very ancient norms. Sartre has not given us a new scale of values; he has simply dusted off and updated what people have been thinking for the last twenty-five hundred years. The specifically philosophical formulation is unimportant. The important thing is that as the champions of values intellectuals enter the lists against the domestic establishment and formulate public opinion in the eyes of the other peoples of the world.

If the intellectuals keep on saying something long enough, it gradually comes to be true! So the world became convinced that American opinion was against the war in Vietnam, as the world was also convinced that French opinion was against the war in Algeria. The people who were for the war were usually not intellectuals and therefore had hardly any available means of making their views known (and when they did speak, they usually spoke clumsily); as far as public opinion was concerned, therefore, these people simply did not exist.

"Do you mean to tell us that there were people who defended the war in Algeria, defended French Algeria?" Within France, yes. Outside of France, world opinion was definitely hostile to France, just as it was to the Vietnam war or to Holland at the time of the war in Indonesia. The people within a country who side with their country's action cannot, however, defend domination, conquest, or exploitation with a good conscience; they may be convinced that these things are necessary, but they do not have morality on their side, and in the West it is essential to have morality on your side.

Outside the given country, on the other hand, a different but equally decisive mechanism comes into play: these others now have a way of creating a good conscience for themselves. Thus, after having itself played the villain at whom the whole world pointed its finger, France courageously sided with the Arabs against Israel, with North Vietnam against the United States, with the black Africans against Rhodesia. The French had found a way of regilding their own tarnished escutcheon, of repairing their own virginity, of restoring their reputation as friends of freedom. It is the influence of bad conscience and of the desire to regain a good conscience that explains how the West has been compelled to favor the peoples of the third world and the socialist world (I am still speaking of public opinion, not real action).

On one side, then (the side of the communist dictatorships), we have opinion that is formulated without any difficulty in a monolithic manner; on the other, opinion that is in fact divided, yet has no choice but to take the same tack as opinion in the dictatorships. This is how "world opinion" is formed (an opinion that has nothing to do, of course, with the opinions of billions of individuals).

To have world opinion on your side is by no means an unimportant thing; in fact, today it is even a guarantee of success. If France was forced in the end to leave Algeria, this was chiefly due to the pressure of world opinion.[11] We ought not to forget that in 1960 there was good reason for thinking that the war was practically over and that the French would win a military victory. The National Liberation Front was very much divided; the National Liberation Army had exhausted its resources. Yet France could not simply restore its colonial domination; that was morally and psychologically impossible. Meanwhile, the whole of world opinion was on the side of the Algerians. France could not but yield to these two facts. As far as I know, this was the first time in history that a conquering people (though their victory was limited, doubtful, and contested) was forced to yield and withdraw.

The same thing has happened often enough since then. Public opinion, thanks to the media, has now become an unparalleled force. It was public opinion (and not just China) that forced the United States to withdraw from Vietnam. It would have been morally impossible for the American government, in the face of world opinion as expressed first and foremost in its own press, to invade Vietnam or even to continue the bombing indefinitely. We ought to bear in mind, too, that the United States itself had in large measure contributed to the shaping of such world opinion by its judgment on the other colonial powers in 1945. World opinion was right, of course: How could anyone not be on the side of the weak and defenseless, of the women and children being crushed by bombardments? We are in the presence here of "immediate data of consciousness." But these "immediate data" were produced by the West; they are an exclusive creation of the West.

For a while, only Portugal and South Africa have been resisting the pressure of world opinion. Now Portugal has given in. What of South Africa? When will the crisis come? It is not possible to go on indefinitely being cursed by all and abandoned by one's own. The same thing has happened in the socialist camp. Russia long stood for unity of principles and action; this was true even in Stalin's time. The break came with the invasion of Czechoslovakia, when "world opinion" suddenly turned against Russia. Hitherto, Russia had been able to do as it pleased; it could count on the support of all the communist parties. It could rely on the conviction of the socialist countries that capitalism stood for everything that was spiritually, morally, and politically evil. In fact, even in those who were not communists, Russia managed to create a bad conscience and thus a kind of unconscious acceptance of its anticapitalist propaganda. Except for the fanatics who remained openly fascist, the other people who were hostile to communism were ashamed of their hostility and did not dare publicize it: morality, after all, and everything good were on the side of the communists![12]

Suddenly, all that changed. More accurately, bad conscience continued to identify communism with morality and the good, but communism was no longer identified with Russia. Frequently, Russia was even accused of having betrayed communism. Since that time, Russia has found itself in the same position as the other great states. It knows it cannot again invade Czechoslovakia, as it had earlier invaded Poland and Hungary.

In this whole matter of world opinion, there is one more factor that we must not overlook: the United Nations. The United Nations can claim to give political expression to world opinion. It does so, of course, in a much less clear and urgent way than the opinion manufactured by the intellectuals, but it does function as a moral point of reference and a source of legitimacy. It is still far more influential, certainly, than the Russell War Crimes Tribunal.

At the same time, we must bear in mind that the third-world nations, which have an absolute majority in the General Assembly, dominate the United Nations. The result is that in any conflict the peoples of the third world are automatically right, no matter what the real causes and conditions may be. The voting in the United Nations is as automatic as in the French National Assembly, and there is just as little likelihood of a surprise in the former as in the latter. Everyone knows in advance how a given deputy will vote because he votes not according to his intellect or his conscience but according to the bloc to which he belongs. It is the same in the United Nations. The western peoples, being a small group, and divided among themselves to boot, are automatically defeated.

It was inevitable, then, that Israel would be condemned, and condemned with a vengeance. But the condemnation did not mean anything, since all that was expressed was the third world's vote in favor of the Arabs, and that vote was a foregone conclusion. To claim that Israel should bow to these United Nations decisions was simply to demand that the alliance of the third-world peoples with the Arabs be considered as representing truth and legitimacy.

It may be said, of course, and with perfect truth, that the United Nations has become completely impotent and incapable of forcing obedience to its decisions. But on the psychological and moral levels, and as far as public opinion is concerned, the decisions of the United Nations count for a great deal, especially when the party found guilty does not obey. Israel lost considerable prestige, even among its friends and supporters, from the fact that it was condemned by the United Nations and did not submit. Israel was now branded as dishonorable, so to speak. Even those frankly favorable to Israel became hesitant and doubtful, less certain that Israel had right on its side; their bad conscience was intensified by the fact that the wretched and exploited third world had sided with the Arabs.

Let us return to our main theme. If we want to know who the truly poor of our age are, we must look perhaps to the attitude of world opinion more than to anything else; or at least we must combine the three factors we have discussed. North Vietnam is not among the poorest nations. Israel, however, by reason of its great isolation, does belong in a sense among the poor nations. No matter what view you take, you must remember that Israel is under constant pressure from an enemy one hundred times greater in numbers; that its territory is completely encircled; that it has been condemned by the United Nations, with all the countries of the third world and the socialist bloc voting against it; that it has been abandoned by a large number of western countries; that it is indeed supported by "international Jewry," which is no little thing but the limits of which can be measured by the loss of many early friends, and partially supported by the United States, but there are many risks and uncertainties about the future of this support.

Despite its military and economic power, then, Israel is a poor nation in respect of world opinion. You can say Israel is a shocking imperialist (this can only refer to Israel's relationship with the United States; how can anyone possibly say that Israel, in itself, is imperialist?); you can say it because it is part of "the worldwide judgment" of Israel (a simplistic, utterly ridiculous judgment, but one that is also convincing and shared by many, and one that determines much else). Given world opinion, you can say that Israel is militarist, statist, aggressive, and a police state.

This last statement is true enough, but how can a nation in Israel's terrible situation help being all these things? I would be very happy if people had the courage to apply impartially the kind of reasoning I hear so often in leftist circles. For example: if guerrillas or the Palestinians take hostages, it is because they have no other way of making their voices heard; they take such extreme measures because they are so desperate. Or again: if the rebels (within our own society) go around vandalizing everything (as in 1968), it is because society first became repressive and violent. Let us apply the same criteria to Israel. Here is a nation that has been subjected to violence since its origin in 1947, to constant aggression, overt or disguised, and that has no other practical means of assuring its survival than arms and an eye-for-an-eye response to attacks. How else was Israel to have survived? (That argument will not convince those who think Israel should not survive, but few have the audacity to say this openly.) In other words, it is the environment that is responsible for Israel becoming a military and police state.

The Palestinians, taken individually, are poor, of course; they are still uprooted, exploited, harried. No doubt of that. They are among the poorest of the poor, and there is no point in recalling, since we have heard it a thousand times, the hunger, the crowding, the lack of work the Palestinians suffered when they were stuffed into the camps in the Gaza Strip.

With regard to the Palestinians, however, two points need emphasizing. The first is that the wretched condition of the Palestinians was only partially due to the action of Israel and the West. The severe life of the camps became permanent only to the extent that the Arab peoples were unwilling to let the Palestinians in, and the Palestinian leaders stubbornly refused to lead their people elsewhere. Yet it was no more difficult for the immense Arab world to accept the Palestinians than it had been for Germany to accept the hundreds of thousands of Germans who were driven from their homes in 1945, or for South Vietnam to accept the hundreds of thousands (perhaps a million) of Vietnamese who fled from the Vietcong regime, or for France to accept a million Algerians. The Palestinian camps are the deliberate, systematic work of the Arab world in its effort to keep an abscess open and maintain a sign of permanent rejection of Israel (the creation of which also led to this injustice). Unfortunately, we live in a world in which one injustice is righted only by creating another. But where would we be if Germany had penned its refugees into camps on the Oder-Neisse line as a protest against that line, or if France had penned the returning French Algerians into camps as a protest against an Algerian Algeria?

The second point is that the Palestinians, because of their courage and heroism, and especially because of the use made of them in the great debate between the powers and between the communist and the American strategy, have now become indispensible pawns. They have become a fixed part of the scene. The world press echoes their claims and expectations. Countless committees of support, the churches, the parties of the Left, the communist states have taken up the cudgels for them. The individual Palestinians, let me repeat, are deeply unfortunate; they have been fed, for the most part, by gifts from the international organizations, and this means by gifts eighty percent of which comes from the United States, the very country against which the Palestinians are used as propaganda. But the Palestinians as a group, as a political entity, have become very important on the world scene. They are supported by all the leading intellectuals, and have gradually won world opinion to their side. Thus, as a group they have ceased to be poor. They have won the victory, and despite their wretchedness, or rather, because of it, they have become the heroes of the age.

They have become heroes also despite the outrages they commit. People excuse everything they do (by "people," I do not mean the corner shopkeeper, who continues to be shocked by assassinations, but whose opinion does not count; I mean the "opinion makers"). On every occasion, world opinion justifies them, whereas when Israel responds in kind, world opinion does its utmost to show up the injustice of Israel. The supporters of the Palestinians thus are in the pleasant position of being on the side of justice and the poor, but also on the side of those who cannot fail to win.

Given the gradual turn in world opinion, Israel cannot but lose in the long run. The longer the conflict lasts, the more Israel's chances of winning lessen. Israel may win ten wars, but the Arab world will still be there, unchanged. Israel need lose only one war, and it will be swept away. Meanwhile, the world is beginning to tire of the whole business: "Let's put an end to it, and, since Israel is the cause of all the trouble, let's eliminate Israel." That is why Israel is poor, and the Palestinians, as a group, are rich. The United Nations has given the Palestinians its blessing.

My main purpose in the next few pages is to remind the reader of all those who have simply disappeared into the secret dungeons of the world's memory. This vast group includes, to begin with, all the peoples who were displaced and conquered after the Second World War: the Poles placed under the Russian and the German yoke, the Germans placed under the Polish yoke, the Balts and the Bessarabians placed under the Soviet yoke, etc. In all, fifty million people had their destiny determined, without their consent, by the victory and the Yalta Conference; the conquerors crushed every protest and revolt. These people were helpless, since world opinion was indifferent to them. They have been left far more abandoned than the Palestinians.

I think here also of the Harki tribe in North Africa. A terrible tragedy, this: a people harried by their fellow countrymen, deserted by the France in whose hands they had put themselves and whom they trusted; forced to flee, since their only choice was death or exile. The Harkis have been forgotten by the world. French opinion on the whole has lost all interest in them because, after all, the National Liberation Front won out, did it not? Besides, were not the Harkis traitors pure and simple? Collaborators as loathsome as the ones who sided with the Nazis? No! The Harkis did not betray their own people; all they did was accept a new form of civilization for them. The Harkis are still the poorest of the poor and abandoned. But, like the other peoples I just mentioned, no one cares about them; that gives us the measure of their poverty. They are no longer a burning issue for anyone. Besides, they have abandoned the fight, and are no longer an embarrassment. If they are now utterly wretched, that is no longer our concern.

Still more remarkable is the refusal of world opinion to be concerned about the peoples still fighting for their freedom; they are still resisting their invaders, but no one is interested. The list would be a long one and might begin with the people of Bihar and with the southern Sudanese. But I shall concentrate on two examples. The first is the Kurds, who have been fighting for their freedom longer than any people in the world today. Their struggle began in 1804; they have been fighting for one hundred and seventy years, almost uninterruptedly, against extremely brutal regimes, being subjected to terrible repression ever since the Turkish conquest.

For a century they fought without ever yielding, and everyone knows the atrocities the Turkish authorities inflicted on the Kurds and the Christians of the Ottoman empire. Yet, since 1920 and 1944 their lot has not been much better. Divided among Turkey, Iran, and Iraq, the Kurds have been subjected to systematic cultural, religious, military, and political repression, especially by Iraq. The Kurds have no right to their own languages; every one of their peaceful demonstrations has cost them hundreds of their people slain (recall the massacres by the Turks at Mardiri and Bayir in 1961). They have been obliged to wage incessant war against Iraq.

What we have in the case of the Kurds is not an ordinary everyday nationalist claim, for in fact a whole culture is at stake. The wish to create a Kurdish nation and state is much less important than the far more radical appeal: "Leave us be; we ask nothing of you; let us speak our own tongue, practice our own religion, stand apart from your political and economic system." There you have the basic issue for these hill people who want to remain genuinely free and not be absorbed into the system of the modern nation-state. That very issue makes the Kurds immensely important, but no one cares. Here you have between two and ten million people claiming their freedom, or rather, asking simply that others leave them the freedom they have up there in the mountains, between two and ten million people complaining only that others will not leave them in peace. But world opinion refuses them a glance or a moment's attention.

When I wrote the preceding two paragraphs in June 1974, the articles of Postel Vinay had not yet appeared in *Le Monde* (they were published in July 1974). But even if I had read the articles first, I would not have written differently. Postel Vinay provides a few descriptions of the struggle, but his whole approach is folkloric and journalistic, interested only in what might be eye-catching; he says nothing about the deeper issue. In fact, in my judgment he even does the Kurdish cause a disservice by his emphasis on the feudal elements in the situation. In addition, he has the struggle begin in 1961, and forgets that this was simply the resumption of resistance that stretches much further back, just as he forgets to say anything about the persecution of the Kurds under the Turkish regime and in Iran. As a matter of fact, the only reason a great newspaper suddenly became interested in the Kurds was because two weeks earlier General Barzani had threatened to destroy the most important petroleum installation in Iraq and to cut off access to the oil reserves. Things were becoming serious! It was a different matter when these backward mountaineers were threatening to aggravate the oil crisis! But their struggle for their freedom, their culture, their identity? Not a word. No one was interested.

In these articles, Postel Vinay, who was incapable of seeing the problem in its entirety, asked what General Barzani really wanted. Would political negotiations not be more profitable in the long run? What was the "wise course of action" in these circumstances? The writer of course made oil the chief consideration, and mistook for the real issue something that for the Kurds was simply a momentary weapon to be used in a long war. Postel Vinay had no inkling that the Kurdish problem is not reducible to the conflict between the Kurds and Iraq. In his mind, once Iran gave aid to the Kurds in Iraq, the Kurds of Iran must have been satisfied. Once again, he confused circumstances with structures, and did not realize that the Iranian Kurds had established a Kurdish state in 1965.

The point I want to bring home is that the Kurds are radically poor precisely because everyone so profoundly misunderstands their struggles and wants at any cost to fit the Kurds into the overall pattern of world politics. For example, a spokesman for the Kurds, Mudhaffer Sheik Kadir (Association of Kurdish Students in France), writing in *Le Monde* (July 1974), calls on General Barzani to regain control by adopting an anti-Zionist, pro-Arab, pro-Soviet position and by putting himself at the head of a socialist movement. What greater betrayal of the Kurds can we imagine than to draw them into the stupid worldwide conflict—especially since in the most recent phase of the Kurdish struggle Russia has been showing itself hostile to the Kurds (October 1974).

In the progressive perspective of Postel Vinay, the Kurds, good fellows though they are, are living in the Middle Ages; they are a holdover from a past era. He notes that "the basic cell, the family, is intact"; how abnormal that must seem to people who have grown accustomed to the paradise of our rationalized world. The Kurds retain their traditions; therefore, they are wrong. They are to be pitied, of course, for the persecution they have undergone, but they must accept progress! It never seems to enter Postel Vinay's mind that the Kurds might be justified in defending their social structure and way of life. Has rational efficiency really produced such brilliant results in the third world?[13]

At this point, a year after writing my original paragraphs on the Kurds, I must add a few lines. Now, for the first time, the Kurds have lost all hope. On March 25, 1975, General Barzani acknowledged that the agreement between Iran and Iraq means that all is over for the Kurds. Deprived of their bases in Iran and of their sources of supplies, and cut off from everyone and everything, the Kurds are virtually eliminated. *Le Monde* now speaks of them as "insurgents" (that tells you which way the wind is blowing). The agreement between Iran and Iraq is a bit of high politics and has been written, as usual, on the backs of the poorest of the poor. Once again, the interests of the mighty have crushed the heroes, but no one is interested in the latter. On the contrary, we hear only congratulations and rejoicing. The Arab world is united, a leftist regime and a rightist regime have been reconciled, the oil-producing powers are in agreement, an Iran that is pregnant with the future is friend once more to an Iraq that is full of resentment: What more do you want? A few million wretched victims? Forget them, forget them.

In any case, a few months from now, when the trap shall have completely closed around the Kurds, no one will even speak of them any more. One hundred and seventy years of struggle will really be over, since, unlike past oppressors, Iran and Iraq, who are no worse than the Turks were (they are much better in fact), have, along with all the other modern states, an unlimited power to liquidate, rub out, and annihilate the minorities in their territories, leaving not a trace of them behind. We have really become much more efficient in this regard. It is only in weak and liberal countries (like the United States) that you hear talk any more of "oppressed minorities." Who says anything of the Kabyles of Algeria, of the animistic tribes of southern Sudan, of the (real) Katanganese, of the Biafrans? They have simply disappeared. In ten years it will be difficult to recapture any memory of who and what the Kurds were. Only the historians will remember, but to no avail.

The Tibetans have suffered the same fate. Tibet is not China, as I said earlier. The takeover of Tibet by the Chinese was a conquest pure and simple, and a difficult one at that.

Here, however, as in other areas, Mao was simply continuing the policies of Chiang Kai-shek, who had begun the conquest of eastern Tibet by gradually occupying the Chamdo area. Mao's conquest was more brutal. Beginning in 1950, an army of one hundred twenty thousand Chinese moved against the eight thousand-man army of Tibet; the Chinese met unexpected resistance, however, and it was only in 1959 that they succeeded in occupying the whole of Tibet. Tibet's appeal to the United Nations had been rejected in 1950, and despite the efforts of the Tibetan government the name of Tibet would not be spoken at the United Nations until 1959.

The Chinese policy in Tibet is one of complete oppression. A major practice is forcibly to remove all the five-year-old children and take them to China; there they stay for over ten years until they are completely Sinified and can be sent back to Tibet to teach their brothers there the truth. The deportation of children is an everyday occurrence. But it should not make us think that Tibet has been pacified. Like the Kurds, the Tibetans have continued to fight the Chinese for over twenty years, and on a large scale. They, too, are fighting for their freedom. It is chiefly the seminomadic hill peoples of the Khamba tribe that are doing the fighting, but, as in the case of the Kurds, the struggle is more than guerrilla warfare in the mountains. There is now a well-organized Tibetan army, and China is forced to keep a permanent force of about two hundred thousand men on the scene, and these are almost constantly fighting. The French did not have many more than two hundred thousand men in Algeria!

Not only is no one interested in the Tibetans; there is even a systematic refusal to notice them. How many people know, for example, that Patterson made an extraordinary filmed report on the Tibetan resistance *(Les Cavaliers du Kham)*, and that this film has been seized wherever the western states have been able to locate it, while in France its showing was prohibited in 1972? Censorship has been imposed, but no one seems at all upset.

The Tibetan cause is certainly as worthy as that of the Palestinians; indeed, the Tibetans are much more utterly poor, since no one, absolutely no one, is interested in them. The cause of the Kurds is as worthy as that of the North Vietnamese; indeed, the Kurds are much more utterly poor, since they lack every vestige of independence and no one is at all interested in these brave people. There is no Committee for the Independence of the Kurds or of the Tibetans; there are no reports on them, no effort to marshal public opinion on their side. These two cases are typical of the way in which individual poverty is matched by collective and political poverty. These people are impoverished when it comes both to economic goods and to international support and fame.

Here we have the truly poor. Why, then, are the generous voices that are constantly being raised in behalf of the American Indians and blacks, the oppressed peoples of Chile and Brazil, and the Palestinians silent about these truly poor? Why did the Russell War Crimes Tribunal say nothing about the abominable actions of the Iraqis and the Chinese? Unfortunately, the answer is, I fear, only too clear.

Take Biafra. No one was interested in Biafra for many years, until someone discovered (or claimed to discover) that the conflict there was a sordid conflict over oil (I distrust this claim completely). Then the Biafran business began to be interesting. Why? Because it was possible at last to apply the simple, universal explanation: the theory of the class struggle, of vested interests at work, of imperialism, the CIA, and all the rest. Then it was worth attending to the Biafrans, in order to condemn them as tools of imperialism. In themselves, they were completely without importance, and their frightful sufferings did not deserve the attention of the lofty political thinkers who create world opinion.

What of the Kurds? Our dear friends, the Arabs, are right, of course. On the capitalist side, the line is: we are not going to aggravate the oil crisis by supporting those scatterbrained hillbillies. The leftist line is that the Arab peoples are presumed right. The Arab nations (except for Faisal's Saudi Arabia and for Southern Yemen) are progressive and are moving along the honorable road of nationalism and socialism.

The Kurds, on the other hand, are reactionaries, a throwback to the Middle Ages; we are not interested in them.

The situation of the Tibetans is even worse. Both the Right (Peyreffitte)[14] and the Left are filled with admiration for China; they are in agreement in their esteem for a regime that has put together the "cultural-economic-political-democratic-spiritual-socialist-humanist-revolutionary" solution. How could anyone be on the side of the obscurantists who refuse the great joys of such a regime? The Tibetans are evidently nothing but slave-owning feudalists (in fact, slavery never existed in Tibet, but what does another lie matter?), who are out to defend their privileges; it is hard to know whether to be hostile or ironic toward such retarded people.

These unanimous reactions make one thing quite clear: our noble defenders of North Vietnam or black Africa have not the slightest interest in the freedom of the peoples involved. They care as little for the Vietnamese and the Africans as they do for the Kurds and the Tibetans. The only thing that matters to them is their political positions, which have been adopted for emotional reasons and without reflection and which have a purely sociological explanation. The Palestinians, the Chileans, the Brazilians simply provide arguments in a debate, themes for propaganda. The reality of their suffering and oppression leaves these good apostles untouched. They will lose interest in these victims (as they did in the Algerians immediately after Ben Bella's victory), once they are no longer useful as a springboard for partisan debate. Do not let yourself be fooled by the outcries of the people who defend the Palestinians, the Chileans, the American blacks. Their words are nothing but the functioning of a simple sociological mechanism. They do not realize it, but they are liars.

The West has unified the world. Western rational, efficient methods have taken over the world. For these two reasons, all peoples now confront one another directly. The world has been shaped by the mass media, a western invention, and the mass media have transformed the meaning and reality of wealth and poverty. In the process we discover another betrayal of the West. In order to win forgiveness from the many peoples outside the West who are now gaining power, the West is betraying the truly poor, walling them up in silence, and helping those whose approbation it seeks to bury them in oblivion.

The truly poor are the minorities we forget about. That is the proper definition of "the truly poor." Where now are those freedom fighters, the Biafrans and the Katanganese? They had to be sullied and accused (as defenders of capitalism and imperialism) with the help of base lies, so that they might be buried still deeper, and their national leaders oppressed and slaughtered. Katanga did not belong to the Congo kingdom of pre-Belgian days any more than Tibet ever rightfully belonged to China. But the Katanganese and the Tibetans were minorities, and the history of the last thirty years allows us to state a general law: ethnic and cultural minorities have no right to independence, must be eliminated, and are always wrong.

A bitter experience, indeed, and a bitter truth. Moreover, it was at the very moment when, in a rather idealistic gesture, the West proclaimed the principle of self-determination for minorities and of independence for "nationalities" that the first massive violations took place: in the Treaty of Versailles and in the Russian takeover of the Ukraine. The ideological scales have not been impartial when it has come to judging between the rights of minorities and the need of forming nations. Nationalism is the universal law of our time; everything else must yield to it. Thus it seemed perfectly normal, at the very moment when the League of Nations was proclaiming its major principle, that Yugoslavia and Czechoslovakia should come into existence as entities made up of oppressed minorities! It seemed perfectly normal that, at the very moment when the Union of Soviet Socialist Republics was proclaiming the free choice of the socialist republics, the central government should crush the movement for autonomy under Makhno.[15]

Proclaiming the independence of minorities was a sure way to stir up rebellion and insubordination. Consequently, a variety of cultures and peoples were condemned, by capitalist and communist regimes alike, in the name of the worldwide nationalist communion. The forgotten national minorities: these are the truly poor. Who defends the Biharis? The Utus? The Muslims of northern Chad? Disappear, troublemakers!—unless, of course, you are pawns the powerful nations can use for their world strategy. Since 1945 there has been a real collapse of the minorities under the twofold pressure of the communist regimes and the nationalist regimes in the newly liberated countries. Of course, by then the work had already been done in any case.

Such has been the drama of our time: the new powers knew of no other road to travel than the road the older powers had traveled before them. This meant eliminating local cultures, crushing movements for independence, accusing those in favor of autonomy. By what seems an astounding inconsistency, the regimes tolerate minorities that come within the range of acceptable political opinion. Capitalist regimes allow communist parties; African regimes allow a number of political "parties"; socialist regimes allow center-leftist parties. In other words, political views that fall within the spectrum of colors that are generally admitted are, strictly speaking, acceptable. But cultural minorities? Absolutely not. It is not admissible that in the name of a common past, a religion, rites, and principles, or a special language and customs, a group should refuse submission to a political organism that is national and seeks to unify by centralizing. World opinion is set; there is no recourse against it. The cultural and ethnic minorities are condemned. Their members are the truly poor of our century.

2   The Shipwreck of the Left

What, from now on, is the position of the Left in regard to the poor, who were the sole justification for the Left's existence? The terrible fate of Makhno was not, after all, an accident, a mistake, a regrettable but forgotten deviation. No, it was the starting point of a development that unfolded with inexorable rigor and brought shame to the Left. Not only that, but it was already written by Lenin into the subtle scheme of strategy and

tactics. He said, as everyone knows, that you must first esti-
mate the chances a revolution has; you must choose whatever
can serve the revolution, ally yourself with whatever forces are
at present deliberately or indeliberately promoting the revolution, and dissociate yourself from those forces that are likely
to militate against the revolution.

The Left, therefore, could condemn the revolt of the Czechs
against Austro-Hungarian oppression. Later on, it could ally
itself with Hitler. At a much earlier date, it could crush the
Spartacists and Rosa Luxemburg.[16] The poor? They are simply a counter on the chessboard, a lever for strategic or tactical
purposes, an army in reserve. If the unemployed proletariat is
the reserve of capitalism, the poor proletariat is likewise nothing more than the manpower pool and the reserve of the
revolution. The revolution has been turned into a kind of
transcendent goddess, and the mere mention of her name
supplies the ultimate reason, the absolute justication, the all-
excusing goal, the meaning and line of demarcation for everything. The poor have no value in themselves; they are not
defended and protected because they are poor, oppressed,
and alienated. The Left is "interested" in the category of the
poor only to the extent that the poor render service to the
great plan and can be made part of it, that is, to the extent that
they accept the role of pawns, of manpower pool, of anonymous troops in a larger unity that is comparable to an army.

The organized Left has turned into the kind of general for
whom the troops are solely a means of winning the battle. The
human reality of the soldier who suffers under him is completely unknown to him. That is exactly the attitude of the Left
to the poor; in this, the Left is only imitating Lenin. On this
point, and this point alone, I disagree radically with the Left.
The trouble is that everything else depends on the right or
wrong attitude to the poor!

The Left has now become as much of a liar and hypocrite
as the bourgeoisie, because it continues to proclaim what it
regards as its own great virtue: the defense of the poor. It
continues to portray itself as representative of the classes that
live in wretchedness, but it is lying. The Left defends and

supports only what can be of service to it, only the people whom it can use for its propaganda or for some form of direct action. It uses the poor exactly the way capitalism does: it exploits them. It leads them along without revealing to them its real objectives. It lies to them day after day.

Need we remind the reader of Monatte's disillusioned exclamation in 1950?[17] We need not ask any of the questions that Sartre the Innocent tragically asked himself concerning the Communist party. All we have to do is look at the reality. But then, Sartre has always, from the very beginning, substituted his imagination for reality. "Tell me, then," you say, "who nowadays in France defends the workers, the immigrants, the unemployed? Are they not the really poor?" Ah, yes, they are the poor whom the Left can currently use in order to attain its objectives, and that is the only reason why the poor are pushed to center stage and taken seriously. They do not exist in their own right; no matter what fountains of tears the intellectuals of the Left may shed over them, the poor exist, in their eyes, solely as examples of exploitation, alienation, and oppression.

Why do I say such shocking things? The answer is simple: the crystal-clear evidence of historical fact makes me say them. When there are many groups that are equally poor and equally oppressed, why does the Left choose to defend only some while not simply forgetting the others, but condemning them, heaping shame and scorn upon them, and making them the object of its hatred? Why? For purely tactical reasons. That is why I say that the poor whose cause the Left champions have no more value in themselves, for the Left, than any other group does. Why is the Left not concerned about the Harkis?

In addition, once a communist regime is established, there are no more poor! Those who rebel suddenly become dangerous counterrevolutionaries who must be crushed. The dreadful state of the peasants in Russia, the wretchedness of the masses in Algeria? No such thing! The same for countless other examples no one could dispute. In a communist regime the poor are wrong to say they are still poor, and to attempt rebellion against this new oppression. That is the great law governing tactics. No one had the right in 1936 or 1945 to say that Stalin's communism was a bloody dictatorship and that the Russian concentration camps were as bad a; those of the Nazis. No one has the right today to say that China is an iron dictatorship and that concentration camps exist aplenty there. Why? To say such things would serve the enemies of the revolution.

The Left is up to its neck in lies. In no sense does it represent the poor; in no sense does it defend them. It has taken from them the religious illusion of a heavenly paradise to come, and given them instead the political illusion of an earthly paradise to come. When it comes to the poor, the Left is in exactly the same position as the bourgeois church of the nineteenth century. It displays the same characteristics and deserves the same contempt. Like the bourgeois Christians of the nineteenth century, the Left distinguishes between the good poor (those who walk in rank, those who are the good sheep of the revolution, those whose situation can be exploited for propaganda purposes) and the bad poor (those who refuse to regard themselves as well off under a communist regime, those who rebel without rhyme or reason, simply because they are unhappy, and without giving heed to the plan for a world revolution, those who represent traditional values and a traditional culture). These bad poor must be simply repressed and suppressed.

From the moment when the Left thus permanently betrayed the poor, it also betrayed the West. It has chosen the path of the total lie; that is, like the bourgeoisie in whose footsteps it walks, the Left is reversing the course that led to the creation of the West. The Left, like capitalism, identifies freedom with its own dictatorship. Reason has been turned into the most insipid kind of sectarian rationalism. The individual has disappeared amid the turmoil of the collectivity. History made by man has been replaced by a divinized history that unfolds in a gloomily automatic fashion. That which was the honor and glory of the West has become, in the hands of the Left, a barren redundancy, a meaningless discourse that will never lead anywhere.

There will be no more singing tomorrows because the Left

has thrown away its inheritance. It has sunk into the most incredible kind of mysticism, and ended in building mythologies that are utterly surprising to anyone who does not begin as a believer. Even the wildest myths built on Christian foundations were models of reason and wisdom when compared to the utterly numbing discourses we used to hear in Stalin's time and are hearing today about Mao's China. When such mysticism prevails, no experience or reason or analysis is of any use. The leftist believer is utterly medieval in this respect, especially if he is an intellectual. And this religiosity, characterized by the infallibility of the party, has brought conformism with it. The Left in our day embodies all the conformisms.

In so doing, the Left again betrays the West. The more it has perverted all the innovations the West gave the world, all the possibilities the West opened up to man, the more it has become the pious inheritor of all the evil the West brought into the world. It will be enough to recall the two great plagues: man's exploitation of his fellow man, and nationalism. Because the Left comes along afterward as the heir, it carries all these mistakes, and the bloodshed they cause, to their logical conclusion. After all, even in the worst period of the African slave trade in the seventeenth and eighteenth centuries, the West never turned man into an instrument of production so utterly without rights and autonomy as Russia has.

How can anyone say, "Ah, no! The Gulag Archipelago is only an accident of history; it is the doing of a madman." What kind of language is that for a leftist? There are no accidents in history, and no individual determines the course history takes. No, the Russia of Stalin is already contained in the thinking of Lenin, and that thinking is still determining things today. China is founded on the same principles.

Only one step is still to be taken: the creation of the happy slave. That was exactly what the slave owners of the Deep South managed to create,[18] and the world of rational efficiency will soon succeed in creating it again. The happy slave exemplifies the supreme law of happiness through well-being, a law that is a bourgeois invention which the Left has taken over. But such a law is also the supreme betrayal of the quest for the

Grail that has typified the West throughout its history. The West: never satisfied, eyes always fixed on a receding horizon, ears open to the call of what has never yet been said and done, soul thirsty for something more, something different. How we have fallen! How we have betrayed our nature!

The Left has carried the exploitation of man to the extreme, but it has done the same for nationalism, which, with unwitting madness, it has been busy spreading throughout the world. A matter of strategy, of course. But no one can foresee everything, and this time the strategy has produced more than the Left bargained for. No one reflected on the frenzy nationalism begets, the frenzy that makes nationalism the West's most fatal invention. Consequently, the Left has gladly danced to the same music, and has now made the entire world nationalistic. Where now is the universalism that the West was aiming at and that communist internationalism made its own from 1850 to 1900? Poor Left, which has repudiated its own discoveries in order to sink into gloomy conformism and to follow the easy path!

But at least the Left defends freedom. Then, tell me, who is arguing today for the freedom of students and for women, for the Coalition for the Defense of Homosexuals and sexual freedom, against the censors? No, here again we must look at the facts. Here, as in all other areas, the Left subordinates everything to strategy. As long as the Left is not in power, it supports all the movements that can bring bourgeois society down. It takes every opportunity, no matter how insignificant in itself, to embarrass the government; at a deeper level, it seeks to foster social anomie as the condition most favorable to its purposes.

However, once the Left gains power, it always and everywhere creates the dictatorship of moral order. This has happened in Russia, in Cuba, in China. Then you hear no more about freedom for women; they must do forced labor like everyone else. You hear no more about the absence of censorship, no more about sexual freedom, no more about homosexuality, and so forth. Instead, you have the application of a very strict moral code that will keep the individual hard at work producing and elicit from him a total, unconditional obedience.

I am quite familiar with all the justifications offered. The order must be a socialist one, because this is now a socialist society; simply by existing in this society, the individual possesses all the freedoms and does not need to ask for any more. But these are just words without any basis in reality; they express only a mystique. The reality is that, once in power, the Left shows its absolute authoritarianism and takes us back into those darkest periods of history from which the West emerged only with difficulty.[19]

In the face of these inescapable facts, we cannot but ask: How could such a change have occurred? How could pure gold change into base lead? I think the answer is that there is one challenge the Left could not meet: the challenge of power; everything else has been the result of this. I have pointed out that the betrayal of the poor, which led in turn to a series of denials and perversions, was connected with a clever working out of tactics and strategy. But tactics and strategy in turn were invented and organized for only one purpose: the conquest of power. Political power as will and idea thus led to the betrayal, even before the power was attained and exercised. How much worse the situation, then, when the Left did reach power! At that moment the gulf yawned open, for power showed the Left and its representatives for what they really were; it revealed their utter inadequacy, spiritual, moral, psychic, doctrinal, intellectual, theoretical, ethical, and human!

Power had ruined Christianity. Later, it brought to light the hypocrisy behind liberalism's good intentions. Now it has done the same for the Left. By bringing power to its highest degree of importance, efficacy, and abstractness, the West thus created the means of its own negation and condemnation. It is this, and not merely the limitations of the Left, that the past half century has been revealing. The unforgivable thing is that the West was warned about this from the very beginning, when Jesus Christ chose the way of nonpower, nonforce, nondomination (rejecting even political domination). Moreover, the Left seemed to have grasped the lesson, for it chose the side of the poor. It saw that the right way to save the West and to preserve the truth of all that had been discovered in the great adventure of man was to take the side of the outcast, the lost, the abandoned, the exploited, the alienated.

This choice, however, should not have been translated into "power to the poor" or the dictatorship of the proletariat or the divinization of the poor.[20] Once that sort of regression took place, all the other betrayals would follow, and follow they did. The game is over now, lost beyond hope, and with the loss of the West, the poor are lost as well.

The Left is incapable of retracing the revolutionary path followed by the West. For in the last analysis (on this point we must be quite clear in our minds), the West came into existence and developed because to each basic discovery—of freedom, of reason, of the individual—there corresponded a revolution. The revolution, however, was always a new one. But in our time and probably henceforth, as I have explained at length elsewhere, revolution is no longer possible.[21]

Without repeating myself, I would like to discuss here two points that I neglected to some extent in the earlier treatments, but that are directly relevant to our critique of the contemporary Left with its impotence and its lack of coherence with western culture. The first point is this: in each instance the revolution has taken place at the level of man's real alienation; the alienation sparked the explosion, and triggered the revolutionary movement. For the past two hundred and fifty years, however, man's alienation has been growing more profound, but that which alienates has become increasingly abstract.

Alienations can be purely external (for example, a prison that alienates a man from society). They can also be purely interior, but operative at a completely unconscious level (thus the driver of a car or the watcher of television can be utterly alienated by the machine, yet continue to regard himself as free and as master of the machine). Between these extremes there can be many intermediate forms: an external alienation that is interiorized; an alienation of the will in another person or a product; an alienation that seems to be a liberation but in fact produces an enslavement; an alienation through being despoiled of the work one produces; an alienation through breakdown of the personality under the pressure of external conditions. These last, the external conditions, are varied: torture, publicity, propaganda, drugs, consumption, capitalism, the big city. In all these cases, we are talking about individuals being alienated.

In every society there is some one kind of alienation that is very common, current, and widespread, and affects all the members of the society. Thus the West has produced pathological conditions that are specifically its own. By this I mean that the affirmations in which the essentials of our culture are summed up are matched by alienating negations. Furthermore, as our civilization evolved, the factors causing alienation became more complex and, especially, more abstract.

We start, then, with quite visible, obvious, directly experienced alienations (the police are a clear cause of alienation, and in their persons we experience the alienation caused by the power of the state). In such kinds of alienation, the cause is easy to determine, for it is apprehended in immediate sense experience. Rebellion against the obvious agent of repression and alienation becomes identical with revolution, because the rebellion enables men to destroy directly what they experience to be the obstacle to self-fulfillment; men have experience of the real obstacle, the genuine cause of alienation, so that to destroy it is indeed to effect a revolution. In such cases, the revolution springs directly from the action of rebelling.

Over the past three centuries, man's alienation has become more profound and increasingly difficult to support. At the same time, however, the causes of the alienation have become more complex and more remote, and are not directly experienced as such. On the one hand, then, men experience the manifestations of alienation, but they do not know how to account for them. On the other hand, there are general mechanisms that effectively cause alienation, but men do not experience them in this role. Only by thinking can we discern them and realize what is going on. This thinking, however, does not spring spontaneously from the action of rebelling; on the contrary, it requires the cold, clear exercise of reason. Revolution has practically nothing to do any more with rebellion.

As a result, the constant rebellions of our time miss the mark, for the rebels are incapable of grasping the real issue. Any revolution, on the other hand, would have to be brought about by those who have the clarity of mind to get at the true cause of alienation; these people, however, are not themselves rebels, they have not the power to set movements going, nor do the masses have any motive for following the thinkers after the latter have given their step-by-step intellectual demonstration of the mechanisms causing alienation. This whole development has gone through three stages. We may say that in the eighteenth century the alienation was chiefly political, in the nineteenth chiefly economic, and in the twentieth chiefly technical, that is, due to the application of rational, effective methods. Let us examine each of these briefly.

In the eighteenth century, alienation was due to the growth of political power, the gradual elimination of local and individual freedoms, centralization, the interference of the central authority in a growing number of areas, the elusiveness of the central authority as far as the ordinary man was concerned, the growth of bureaucracy, the increased burdens laid on the majority. Mousnier is certainly right in viewing this political situation as responsible for most of the rebellions and revolutions of the seventeenth and eighteenth centuries.[22] Those who rebelled against the "tyrant" were not mistaken in their target. Of course, the real tyrant was not poor Louis XVI, but the state whose figurehead he was. In any case, the tyrant was both an individual and a discernible power. Similarly, it was easy to start a revolution against Hitler, since it was quite clear who had to be killed.

Yet the response to tyranny was shot through with ambiguity because of the confusion between a survival and a new reality. The new reality was the state, which was already highly abstract and inherently oppressive. The survival was the tyrant, or the image of the tyrant: that is, an individual who acted simply as he pleased and therefore created unhappiness and injustice. Without catching sight of the new organism, rebels rose against the ancient image and, in so doing, effected a revolution, since the problem was in fact one of political alienation. The revolution failed, however, because it permitted a new apparatus of state to be born. The tyrannical individual was eliminated, but there continued in existence a power much more alienating than the tyrant had ever been. We can say, then, that the diagnosis of political alienation was correct, since the whole problem could really have been resolved by an institutional change. At the same time, however, we become aware of how difficult it is to effect a revolution against an abstract structure.

In the nineteenth century, the mechanisms causing alienation changed considerably, since the essential alienation was now economic. It was due to the capitalist organization of the economy and, consequently, to the necessity of producing a profit and to the set of mechanisms geared to a maximum profit. Here the problem is evidently much more abstract and difficult to pinpoint. We are no longer dealing with the capitalist villain of old. We are no longer faced with the opposition between the individual and the moneylender or the owner, both of them persons whom everyone knew and who were the direct causes of human wretchedness. To stop there would be to leave untouched the general mechanism that produced economic alienation. Killing the moneylender or the owner does not effect a revolution.

Marx has given us a splendid demonstration of how abstract the system of economic alienation is. But when it came to effecting a revolution, three difficulties arose. The first was the one I mentioned a moment ago: the survival of an ancient image. People were still thinking in 1850 that the revolution must be the prolongation and continuation of the revolution of 1789, that is, a revolution against a political tyrant. I analyzed this difficulty in my book *Autopsy of Revolution.*

The second difficulty lies in the increasing dissociation of the feeling of rebellion (I am wretched) and the abstract objective of any possible revolution. It is becoming very difficult, if not impossible, to correlate the two. The third difficulty is that of elaborating a long-term strategy for changing the economic structure; such a strategy must itself be abstract, since the economic forces causing the alienation are abstract. The countless problems relating to the strategy, tactics, and organs of the revolution (especially the role of the Communist party, its organization, its relation to the proletariat) spring directly from these three difficulties.[23]

Just as economic alienation made its appearance when political oppressions had already become consciously felt and were the chief object of revolutionary energy, so today economic alienation persists even though the main source of alienation is now to be found in another sphere. For, in the twentieth century alienation is not chiefly and essentially economic but is the result of the growth and spread of technique.* In a sense we have gone beyond the capitalist stage, but alienation is cumulative, each older alienation persisting but in a new form. Thus, in the nineteenth century political alienation still existed but it was included in, dominated and restructured by the mechanism of economic alienation; political power was still a cause of alienation, but it now took the form of the bourgeois capitalist state. So too, at the present time, political and economic alienation still exist, but they are included in, dominated by, and restructured within technical alienation. Technique has thoroughly permeated the structure of the state and the economic structure; political power and the economy continue to be causes of alienation, but in the form now of the technicized state and the technicized economy.

Technique is the present cause of man's enslavement. It is

*[Ellul's use of *technique* and *(société) technicienne* continues to create difficulty for the translator, since "technology" is not usually an adequate rendering of technique as he understands it, while "technique" and "technical" for the noun and adjective respectively can be quite misleading. It should be sufficient to recall Ellul's "Note to the Reader" in *The Technological Society* (New York: Alfred A. Knopf, Inc., 1964): "The term *technique,* as I use it, does not mean machines, technology, or this or that procedure for attaining an end. In our technological society, *technique* is the *totality of means rationally arrived at and having absolute efficiency* (for a given stage of development) in *every* field of human activity."—Tr.]

not simply that, of course. Hypothetically, technique could be wholly a cause of man's liberation, just as, hypothetically, the state could be the source of security and justice, and the capitalist economy could be the source of happiness and of the satisfaction of needs. But all that is hypothetical. In reality, the state, the economic structure, and technique have been sources of alienation.

Man now feels dispossessed of himself. But it is a quite different sense from what he had in the days when he was oppressed from without by a visible material power. The economic society Marx described was more complex than the political society Montesquieu had described before him, and technical society in turn is incomparably more complex than the economic society of the nineteenth century. The causes and mechanisms of alienation have now become completely abstract. The person who feels alienated cannot point his finger at what provokes this feeling, because the causes are legion and their deleterious effects are infinitely refined. This is why when people try to name a cause of alienation, they say something like "consumption" or "entertainment." But "consumption" is just a symbol, since consumption has no independent existence. Moreover, it is a symbol that no longer says anything to the average man. It takes a lengthy process of thought to reach an understanding of how consumption alienates. People are not wrong when they give you a sharp reply: "Don't tell the poor who can't consume that consumption is alienating!" We have no direct apprehension, no direct experience of these causes (our only experience of them is one at several removes of reflection). And yet the modern kind of alienation goes much deeper than the earlier kinds (precisely because the former is much more abstract), just as the alienation caused by economic mechanisms had gone deeper than the alienation caused by the tyrannical exercise of power. It is because of the increasing extent and depth of alienation that Marx endeavored to work out a general philosophy of history, the world, and man. In our own day, as I have been saying, alienation has only increased and deepened.

Alienation today is no longer a matter of being dispossessed of the value produced by labor. It consists, rather, in a breakdown of the personality, a dispersal of needs and capacities, a reduction (in the sociological sense) of the person, a schizophrenia, a diversion of goods, a disappearance of the autonomous center of decision. In short, alienation now touches man at his deepest level. Consequently, it is at that level that the revolution must take place. A revolution that changes economic or political structures or a revolution that destroys a group of men (enemies, oppressors) is now utterly inadequate, since it takes place outside the actual area of alienation.

The trouble is that those who plan and seek to bring about a revolution are still preoccupied with images proper to the near and remote past. They still think that the problem is the bourgeois state or the capitalist economy, whereas in fact the problem is now situated in an entirely different realm. Since man has been attacked and dismantled as an individual, the revolution we need must take place within man himself and not in structures. We need what some would call a change of ideology, but in fact it goes a good deal deeper than ideology, for everyone must discover or rediscover a new factor that is both individual and collective.

Various writers have given us obscure glimpses of this new factor. Thus Edgar Morin speaks of the human paradigm (though I think he is on the wrong trail). A more promising line of thought is provided by Georges Friedmann when he speaks of "wisdom," or Bertrand de Jouvenel when he proposes "amenity," or Ivan Illich with his "conviviality," or Radovan Richta with his "capacity for creativity," or I myself with "individuality."[24] All these suggestions may seem to be old hat, a return to the moral virtues or concepts of a bygone age. In fact, however, they tell us the level at which the real problem exists. Moreover, the only revolution possible is one that takes place precisely at that level. It therefore includes a radical rejection of all ideologies that are destructive of the individual and the subject, and of all the methods that claim to bring objectivity into the human sciences (such methods as structuralism and neo-linguistics) but in fact are based on an anti-individual, antisubject ideology. In short, the revolution must include a radical rejection, not of technique as such, but of the ideology of technique. In my view, the Left has not even begun to travel this road.[25] Quite the contrary! All the more so since the Left is a composite of bits and pieces.

This last remark brings us to my second reflection on revolution, the second of the two points that, I said above, I had neglected to some extent in my earlier treatments of revolution but that are directly relevant to our critique of the contemporary Left. The reflection is this: if we analyze the effective revolutions that have taken place in the past, we find that each of them was unified around what we might call a "leverage point." Each great revolutionary movement had its leverage point, which was formed by bringing together a value (in which a very large part of the population believed) and a social group that already played an indispensable role in its society. The revolution depended on the will of this social group to organize the society wholly in terms of the value in question. The group was a cohesive one, and its cohesiveness gave unity to the revolutionary movement. There was also a coherent interpretation of all phenomena, and this coherent interpretation effected a kind of mutation of the reigning social myth.

Such a conjunction of group and value seems to me to be indispensable if a revolutionary movement is to exist. We may say that in the eighteenth century the leverage point was the conjunction of the bourgeoisie and the value of freedom. In the nineteenth century, the leverage point was the conjunction of the proletariat and the value of justice. In these situations, the value is neither an ideological justification nor a superstructure. What it does is give the group the motivation required for transforming it into a revolutionary group. Marx was wrong in thinking that this transformation could be effected by a simple passage from the objective to the subjective, by men becoming aware of their condition, by intellectual demonstration, and by the objective interplay of a set of forces and relations. No, it is the value that creates the leverage point, when it is assimilated to and by a group that identifies itself with the value.

The trouble today is that there is no value that is assumed

by a cohesive group. The old values are obviously incapable of rousing anyone at all, since people no longer believe in them. There is no comprehensive interpretive doctrine or positive value that any group has taken over. There are only spasmodic agitations in connection with one or other belief that has no future and no acceptable content. As for groups, they form and break up because they exercise no indispensable social function and because they have no internal cohesion. The groups offered us as revolutionary—whether it be third-world groups or the American blacks or "the young" or the migrant workers—are really not revolutionary at all; all they can produce are incoherent outbursts of rebellion and violence that do not in any sense lead to a revolution.

I have tried to show that the restoration of the individual is the needed value, but there is no social group to take it over and identify with it. Its only adherents are a few liberal intellectuals and reactionaries who hear in the term "the individual" a language they think familiar. Not only is the Left not in a revolutionary situation; it cannot even grasp the analysis I have been offering. It continues to speak a language that has no relation to reality; it constantly harks back to the same old formulas and speaks endlessly of socialization, class struggle, nationalization, equalization of incomes, and the like. It does not realize that we are no longer living in the year 1880, and that while all that sort of thing did have a meaning and should still be brought about, it is no longer, in the slightest degree, the answer to our current problem.

It is a fact that the Left no longer makes any claim to be revolutionary. It has buried the revolution and is calmly getting ready to take and keep power. We must go a step further and say that not only is the Left no longer revolutionary, but it now has a very specific and quite different role: its function in modern society is to prevent the revolution. The radical Left, including the Communist party and the United Socialist party, has been tacitly delegated by the entire social body to see to it that no revolution can take place. The parties of the Left and the trade unions are now the best guardians of the establishment. You need but reflect that if these parties attain power it can only be thanks to the working of present institutions. Consequently, they will be very careful to preserve these institutions.

I am not saying, of course, that there is an explicit connivance between society as a whole and the Left, or a clear formulation of the role the Left is to play. The bourgeoisie still pretends to be quite afraid of the Communist party—but how reassuring that nice Communist party is! No one fears it any more, and the bourgeoisie is fully aware that from now on they can have an understanding with it. Just make a show of being afraid of it, and the idea that it is a party of opposition and revolution will be credible. What this means concretely is that the forces of rebellion that exist in the society will be fixated on, catalyzed by, and locked into the Communist party, and will therefore not break out uncontrollably at some other point.

The Left has thus become the great antirevolutionary lightning rod. When François Mitterrand during his campaign used every possible argument to reassure the bourgeoisie, he was not simply using tactics or being hypocritical; he was simply telling the truth. The present antirevolutionary character of the Left seems to me to have two causes, which we have already met: its inability to recognize the basic problems of our contemporary society, and its demagoguery.

The political analysis offered by the Left is now hopelessly out of date and strictly meaningless in relation to the real social and technical structure of our society. Its deficiency is due not so much to an inability to see what is going on, as to the fact that the Left reads reality through an inadequate interpretive grill. When a text is confused, you will never succeed in reading it unless you use the grill that was used in composing it.

The error of the Left is not simply intellectual, however. The Left has a large clientele, and when it makes a false analysis, it turns all its followers in the wrong direction. But when you fix someone's attention on a false problem, you make him concentrate his energies and attention and imagination on it;

thus you prevent him from seeing the real problem and trying to solve it. Because of its revolutionary proclamations, its claims to power, and its repeated statements that, since all problems are political, it is essential that the Left fill the office of President of the Republic, the true role of the Left is now to channel the energies of the people into these questions, to make the people believe the myth that the real causes of suffering will be eliminated when the Left takes power, and thus to turn attention away from any investigation of the true causes. The Left is preventing men from opening their eyes wide and seeing for themselves the real situation. It causes the proletariat to go on living in a mythical universe that has no relation to reality. This is all the easier for the Left to do, since, as we have seen, the true causes of alienation are more abstract and therefore more difficult to discover. In such conditions it is easy to believe the moon is made of green cheese. The politicians of the Left dream only of gaining power; meanwhile, they play the part of puppeteers in a sham theater.

The second reason the Left is now antirevolutionary is its demagoguery. The Left has taken over every commonplace, every platitude, every trite slogan, provided it will attract a clientele. It prostitutes itself with disconcerting ease, showing itself willing to accept allies from every side and money from every hand. Such an attitude can win elections, but it cannot start a revolution. Instead, it takes all the energies and groups that might be revolutionary, and amalgamates them so that they are inevitably absorbed and rendered sterile; then their sole function is to justify the status quo in the name of a revolution that will never happen. The groups that the Left thus integrates into a composite whole act as a façade pointing to a reality that no longer exists but of which men continue to speak. Thus the Left is, in practice, counterrevolutionary.

But if this is so, why do I spend time, in a book on the West, going back over questions of revolution that I have dealt with elsewhere? The answer is that the revolutionary spirit is a basic trait of the West. The West has always advanced by way of revolutions. It was led to do so by the profound contradiction within itself that I attempted to describe earlier. Moreover, the forces it unleashed—secularization, or the advent of the individual, for example—could, in the last analysis, find expression only in this way. The whole movement of the West implies revolution, and the western civilization is the only one to have experienced revolution in depth and as a recurring phenomenon.

With the rise of the West, we pass historically from the assassinations of sovereigns that were a universal practice, and from outbursts of popular wrath, to a much more radical and unique way of challenging society. Nowhere else in the world —in Africa or Asia or America—did anyone invent revolution. We must keep in mind that the three great revolutionary movements in China since the nineteenth century have been directly inspired by the West. Compare, on the one hand, the countless popular riots in China from 300 B.C. to the nineteenth century, or the overthrows of dynasties caused by invasions or palace intrigues, and, on the other, the revolutions of the nineteenth and twentieth centuries, and you will see that with the latter you are in a different world. The revolutions in China have followed the western model.

The West alone committed itself to this perilous road, and that is why I regard the Left as so tragically sterile. It is today betraying the legacy left by the western world. It is betraying the discovery of man and of freedom. The only acceptable revolution that could now come to grips with the new situation would be a tireless retrieval of what the West discovered through practice and project and tried to formulate in a theory. If the Left were playing its proper role, it would be promoting life, freedom, and the individual. No one but the Left can renew that movement, and this is why our situation is so tragic. All those who claim to draw inspiration from the West are in fact rejecting what the West brought into the world. The Right, the conservative movements: these can do nothing. Consequently, when the Left betrays the West to the degree it has today, it seems that western history cannot possibly continue. In fact, history in its entirety seems finished.

For the movement of history to continue, there must be a radical challenging of the state (the political order and the party) and of technique, both of which are inventions of the West. To engage in such a dialectical process and negate each of the West's affirmations, each of the West's discoveries, would be to go back and follow the same path that led to those affirmations and discoveries. The very process is one that the West contributed to the world. The condition, then, that must be met if the course of history is to continue, is that there be a Left that will follow the direction established by the great lines of western thought (and of western thought alone).

That is also the condition that must be met if the peoples of the third world are to rediscover their identity. It is an illusion pure and simple to believe that these peoples are now autonomous, that the future is in their hands, and that the center of history is now located among them. I am not denying their importance or indulging in a simplistic Europo-centrism. I am saying only that the future of man and mankind is still, and will continue to be, determined in the accursed West. The rest of the world might look on with sympathetic good will, but in any case it will not understand the real issue.

If the revolution is to come, there must be a Left that is capable of the reason, individuality, and freedom so cruelly lacking in today's Left. Such a Left will not come into being, however, nor will western history resume its course, unless the Left abandons the "Marxism" that has been so totally distorted and degraded since the death of Marx (and down to Althusser[26] and Mao inclusive) by all those who have decked themselves out in it and exploited it and turned it into a tool, an apparatus, a machine, a utopia, a philosophy, a pseudoscience, in short the gigantic acronym for all our modern lies. The predicament of the West, and therefore of the whole modern world, is not due to Marx but to the exploitation of his work and to the facile conviction that he said the last word. No one has said this last word! We must continue the course of history, but history can henceforth have but one possible direction: to pursue what the western world dreamed and then created.

There is but one tiny light left in the darkness thrown over the world by the betrayal of the Left (which means death for the West). There is but one tiny protest (in the etymological sense of the word: "testimony uttered in the face of . . ."), and it comes from those who want to contest (again, in the etymological sense: "to join in bearing witness"). Theirs is the only hand raised to save the western heritage. Of course, if these contestants were aware of what I am saying, they would reject such an interpretation of them: Do they not cry aloud their disgust with everything western? They do indeed, but that is because they are ignorant of the magnificent treasure that is theirs. Only a few leftists are fighting the good fight, but they are the authentic leftists. Yet, what an ironic situation!

These leftists are the only ones with the courage to proclaim that certain requirements are essential (they are often mistaken, and I do not claim that their thinking and explanations are adequate). They have had the courage to talk again of freedom after the Left had banned the word from its vocabulary because they identified it with bourgeois liberalism and regarded it as contrary to genuine equality. These leftists have had the courage to talk again of man, after such talk had been barred because the scientists had proved that man does not exist. These leftists have engaged in a basic and comprehensive critique, and by doing so have in effect begun to follow the path that led to the creation and invention of the West. This is what they have been doing, even while perhaps thinking that they were representing the East and its yogas and its inward-looking contemplation.

Of course, even though there has been a recovery of some fundamentals, this does not prevent great divergences from immediately showing themselves. Some leftists want to follow the path of reason (the Trotskyites, the anarchists), while others have launched out into the irrational. The important thing, however, is not that their ideas are confused and difficult, and impossible to mold into a theory. The important thing is that these leftists are not theorizing at all: they are living out, and want to live out, what they proclaim. This is why there are divisions and quibblings, all the more since, despite their ideas on community, these people are frankly individualist. If it is difficult to agree on doctrine, how much more difficult to agree on how these great basic orientations are to be embodied!

In any case, these leftists are pursuing the very course the West followed from its beginnings. They are now the ones afflicted with a bad conscience, the ones engaged in self-criticism and in the pursuit of the absolute. I know that in saying this I will make many of them tremble with rage, but that is because they do not grasp the deeper truth of the culture they have inherited. These leftists mark a new stage in our culture. But, they are not the Left! Not by any means! They are the ones the Left has rejected!

CHAPTER III

THE BETRAYAL OF THE WEST

The West has been betrayed: those it persuaded and converted to its cause have now turned its weapons against it. The West has been betrayed: its own children now heap sarcasm and insult upon it, and no one, even if he be still willing to think of himself as a European, will accept now the accusation of being a "Westerner." But in fact the West has betrayed itself. For what is going on at present is really the fruit of a very lengthy process in which everything has been turned upside down, a process in which each conquest has exacted its harsh price, then only to be perverted. For example, we mentioned in passing that the language of reason has caused the irreparable loss of myth and the capacity for creative evocation. Surely a heavy price to pay!

Far worse, however, is the fact that, as progress was made, the West found it impossible to remain at the heights of greatness it had created. Everything was perverted, everything was carried to extremes, whereas the real need was for the greatest possible self-control and moderation. The freedom the West had discovered caused the enslavement of other peoples and, in the West itself, the enslavement of the workers. What a terrible curse! Freedom thus led not only to crimes but to the very opposite of itself. That is why no one could any longer take that freedom seriously, but could only regard it as a lie, an illusion, a hypocritical declaration of principle, under cover of which the strongest could do as they pleased. Surely an example of perversion if ever there was one.

Reason has turned into narrow-minded rationalism, while claiming simply to pursue its own logical end—but that really means: to go to extremes. Again, an odd reversal. Reason that is essentially linked to moderation would beget the immoderation of all-devouring, exclusive, authoritarian, ill-tempered, inquisitorial rationalism! Reason that is essentially linked to clarity would plunge men, by way of scientism, into a confused world of primordial beliefs. Convulsive extremes have replaced moderation and measure. As though a secret curse were at work, everything the West invented and set in motion has been perverted from its true nature. We have here moved far beyond class struggles and sociological interpretations. The fact is that the West aimed at too high a perfection and attained power instead. That is its ultimate tragedy.

1 The Betrayal of Reason and History: The Utopist, the Geometer and the Technician[1]

Reason, which the West invented, has been betrayed. We can distinguish three stages or degrees in the betrayal, and we can dispose of the first two very quickly, since they are well known.

In the first stage, reason engendered rationality. *Ratio,* the Latin word for "reason," meant "measure." Rationality took pride in measuring everything. Its aim was to subject everything to reason, to absorb everything into a rational framework, and to accept no refusal, no overlap, no area of darkness. The unweighable and the unmeasurable were no longer to exist. Reason, which was to provide exact measurement of the self and serve to prevent mental confusion, became instead the source of a new mode of being, measurability. Only what can be weighed or numbered or measured exists. But is it not evident that the little word "only" contradicts reason? Reason was meant to be the measure of man's unmeasurableness, the rein on his hybris, the straight line that could be walked. It was to be the compass, chart, and sextant that would enable the captain to plot the right course for his ship, but it was not meant to deny the unpredictable wind that pushes the ship forward! On the contrary, if reason were to be itself, it must suppose the constant action of the underground forces that give it being and keep it honest, and the existence of the fountain whence the stream of possibilities flows forth. Yet, exalted by the discovery of this marvelous tool, man went to extremes and denied the very thing that gave him life!

The absolutism of rationality was, however, accompanied by an even worse perversion, rationalism. This marks the second stage in the betrayal of reason. With rationalism we pass over into the universe of myths and beliefs. Oddly enough, though, reason became the god of this world. That is to say, man now began to adore the very thing that in the normal course did away with or at least challenged every form of adoration. Rationalism thus made reason the object of belief and gave a mythical dimension to that which is the opposite of myth. Like all religious thought, however, rationalism became incoherent, constricted, sectarian, and narrow-minded. Nothing could be pettier than the rationalists of the nineteenth century. In them, reason, which means openness and self-control, became exclusive of all else and rejected, a priori, anything that did not have a rational side to it.

There is no need to dwell on these first two stages; they have been denounced time and again, and constantly crop up in critiques of the West. The third stage, however, deserves our attention today because of the success utopianism has enjoyed and the erroneous understanding people have of it.[2]

Utopias are presented today as either an anarchic ideal or a reaction against the rationalist mentality. How often we have been told about this dream aspect of utopia, the romantic longing for another world that does not exist, and about how the idea of utopia stimulates the unbridled imagination! "Everything is possible in utopia. Imagine anything you want to: you can throw yourself out into the insubstantial clouds and find treasures there. Our technicized thinking needs this kind of rejuvenating bath, this rational madness. Our conformism needs the sharp reminder contained in this kind of critical nonconformism. More's *Utopia* was a denunciation of England. In our own day, when absolute technique seems to have a tight grip on our world, we need the stimulus of utopian thinking so that we may break out of our technicized universe."

Nothing could be more delusory or hypocritical than such talk as that. Why? Because utopia has never been that kind of thing at all! Utopia is not a world for the unbridled imagination; it is not even a new and different place. Utopian discourse could never have been within hailing distance of anarchy. On the contrary, utopia is "a perfect city, built according to a strict mathematical logic and subject to the demands of total planning. It foresees and eliminates the least loophole and the least challenge to itself. Utopianism and totalitarianism are synonymous." This definition given by Laplantine fits what utopia has always been.

In dealing with utopia we must first decide what our point of reference is. One possibility is to speak of utopia on the basis of the utopias that have been thought up in the course of history, from Plato to Charles Fourier and others.[3] If these are what you mean by "utopia," you are speaking purely and simply of absolutist dictatorships based on the undeviating application of rational scientific methods; in these schemes, the individual is completely denied and fused into the social whole, and everything outside this little world is excluded.

Another possible approach eliminates reference to these historical creations, but the result is murky discourse in which you can say anything you want about utopia. "Utopia" then becomes a word without any content except the stream of words produced by the given writer. But if there is no objective reference, why use the word "utopia" at all? It is not by chance, I think, that men like Henri Lefebvre choose it, for there is a basic mechanism, though subtle in its operation, that leads to the choice of the word. We may describe it briefly as follows.

We now live in a technicized world created by rationalism, and we are increasingly conscious of its dangers. We need a way out of it. It is not possible, however, to give a precise answer to our present world or to find a precise way out of it or to make a satisfactory forecast of a future that would be acceptable. What do we do, then? We throw ourselves into an unforeseeable future; we overleap the intellectual difficulties and build ourselves a city that is not real but is also not a pure product of science fiction. We claim to be creating something revolutionary because we introduce an element of "dream" into it; we leave behind technique and technology, evoke various possibilities—and call the result a "utopia." But the word is not chosen at random, because it allows us not simply to contradict our technicized world. Why so? Because all the utopias ever excogitated have been triumphs of technique, and what the modern utopist unwittingly creates is a radically *technicized* world! Only the visible, striking drawbacks of technique have been eliminated; in reality the utopia represents, in the guise of a dream, the unqualified triumph of technical rationalism. The supposedly revolutionary imagination produces, in fact, an idea that is as antirevolutionary as anything could possibly be. And *that* is why the word "utopia" is used.

A utopia, then, is the most monotonous and boring of all possible worlds. It is "the logical charter for the established order or, better, organization; it is marked by the closed in, smug obviousness of perfect order, expurgation, and foresight."[4] There can be no greater mistake than to think of a utopia as manifesting exuberant imagination, for it is, on the contrary, dry and shot through with peremptoriness. The people in it are completely mechanized. It is precise and meticulous; it is "social rationalism" pure and simple being offered us as the only way to fulfillment.

What is here offered to us as perfection is in fact total planning and the narrowest kind of moralism; utopia is Lewis Mumford's Megamachine at work. Each individual is reduced to being a tiny cog in a whole that functions perfectly because all obstacles have been removed, whether they are the obstacles created by memories (utopia is a world in which history has been abolished; there is no past) or by plans (utopia knows of no new and different future; tomorrow can only be a repetition of today) or by desires (there is nothing to desire in utopia, because every contingency has been foreseen for the common good; any desire on the part of individuals would disturb this perfect mechanism). The individual has completely disappeared and given way to a seamless geometrical pattern. That is what our fine modern utopists want, even though they do not realize it. They want social perfection once and for all, and mathematics alone can give them the certainty they need.

"Utopists abhor what the poets love: the fauna and the flora, the trees that send their branches outward in such an unpatterned, capricious way, the bridges and the streams, and the untamed instincts of men." As Gaston Lafarge has perceptively noted, utopists prefer the square and compass, account books, syllogisms, and taxonomies.[5]

They hate what differentiates, for they are utter conformists in every detail. We must also bear in mind that, sociologically, utopias always originate in the propertied classes, the bourgeois who have been frightened by the undisciplined agitation of revolutionaries. Utopias have a quite specific function: to preserve the status quo, even while pretending to aim at a perfect society, which should silence the agitators. Utopias comfort the way a mother comforts her child: by anticipating and organizing everything and by allowing all the human tendencies to express themselves, provided that they do so in a completely disciplined way and in complete subjection to moral rule. In other words, the tendencies which the individual may express will no longer be his own but those of the abstract social man whom the utopists project. Everything will work out fine, on condition that the individual is so interiorly disciplined that there is nothing personal left of him. There will evidently be no family, no special relation between man and woman, no private property, but neither will there be a private life or sentiments peculiar to the individual. Poetry and music are excluded, because these stir the imagination and may thus lead to major new disturbances. Religion is also excluded and replaced by a thoroughly uniform moral code and an ideology based on a completely abstract human nature. Utopia is characterized by organization gone mad, as the social group is wrenched from its natural environment and remodeled from top to bottom according to requirements essentially urban in nature. . . . Utopists have an incredible plan to reduce the human being to the citizen, and to attach this citizen inseparably to his city, like a nursling who is never to grow up but is forever to remain dependent on his mother.[6]

The dweller in utopia is a perpetual child, protected by a maternal society and behaving with the seriousness and tranquillity that are expected of him. He is not allowed to be distinct from others in any respect; all utopias aim at the perfect identity of all members. Utopia is also cut off from the outside world, for the latter can only be a source of disorder and introduce an uncontrollable factor into the ideal city. Citizens have no right to travel; just think of the people they might meet, and all the dangerous notions they might bring back with them!

Given this ethos, utopia is built on a fanatical trust in schooling and pedagogy. A society completely schooled, in which everything is learned collectively, even how to make love: Does this not remind us of what our own society is becoming? Let us not forget that the most advanced movement always represents the cutting edge of the process of social integration. I am thinking here of the movement of universal sexualization, of collective sexual education, of sexuality in the schools, and so on. How can we fail to see that this whole thing is an effort to eliminate the mysterious, adventurous, uncertain, mythical element in sex and to reduce sex either to cold knowledge or to a practice that is collectivized and therefore technicized?

When the question of sexual education in the schools or of sexology comes up, just listen to the incense-bearers talk of the sexual freedom we are thereby gaining. Listen to them say, as though they had won a great victory: "Now at last we can talk without shame or fear of what people did not dare whisper twenty years ago. See how far we have come! We have got rid of a frightful complex, and have become bold and intelligent. An absurd moral code used to have us tied hand and foot, but now we have destroyed it. We're done with all the complexes and all the false shame. Our dear little children must learn to practice sex right out in the open, just as they openly suck at their mother's breast."

You wicked fools, you cretins who promote sexology and sex education and universal sexualization, have you still not understood what they did to Racine by mumbling about sex to him in school? You have still not understood that school and what they call education for life make the child utterly and forever disgusted with what they do in it, and that the infantile scientistic rationalism that holds sway in the schools will never be improved by introducing experimental sex into the program. If that is done, the only result will be that sex will be trivialized, collectivized, made ridiculous and deadly boring, and stripped of its mystery and drama and passion.

"But that is just what we want: a sexuality that is stripped of its mystery and drama! Why should the human being wax enthusiastic just because he or she has organs for servicing others?" But do you not realize that man needs mystery and passion? That if the white Mass is put into French and turned into a rationalized social affair, he will invent black Masses for himself? That dreaming is no less important, basic, and decisive for man than reason, or rather, that reason ceases to exist if there is no dreaming, no lightheaded imagination, no myth and poetry? Reason then turns into its opposite: rationalistic mathematics.

What you are preparing the way for with your sexology is a human being who is disgusted with sex, who will no longer have the slightest idea of what love is, and who will be even a little more fed up with things than he is now. And, by heaven! we all know what happens when a human being gets bored, jaded, fed up: he finally commits suicide. Your sex education in the schools is training a generation of torturers who will end in suicide. You are taking from them the passion of love (not just sexual love, though that is included), but then they will develop a passion for death. Those are the only two passions possible. What frightful hypocrites you are, claiming to liberate the male by carefully washing out the labyrinthine ways of his heart with a bleach, and the female by washing her sexual organs with the same to make them sterile!

I am not speaking here in the name of morality. In fact, it is precisely against your scientistic morality, which would make everyone a cog in the social machine, that I am raising my voice. (Note that leftist sexuality has exactly the same aim. It is ludicrous to see the battle lines drawn between the learned sexologists with their medical degrees who speak objectively about the matter, and the little sex-liberation groups that profess to be down-to-earth and have no use for theory: the two are doing exactly the same thing!) It is possible effectively to reject this morality, however, only if we can point to a new and different individual manner of acting that does not result from schooling or pedagogy or collective experimentation, but originates in experience that defies adequate expression, in the quaking violation of taboos, in the conflict with pressures from the collectivity, and in the penetration of what was hitherto hidden from one's eyes because it is a realm of mystery.

The human being who lives unsurrounded by this vast shadowy zone is nothing but an insect on a white wall. It is his nature to go forward while he, and he alone, throws out the light he needs. If you set him on a wall that is already clean and whitewashed and offers no problems, he has nothing to do and no reason to go on living. So, with your good intentions you are preparing a fine air-conditioned hell and a fine generation of human beings who are utter conformists and lack all desire to live. And it is here that we reach the very heart of every utopia. Every utopia claims to be an expression of freedom when in fact it is a barracks pure and simple. It claims to be an obvious method of achieving happiness when in fact it is a gigantic school dedicated to instruction and has all the defects of the most boring school possible. It is all-controlling, authoritarian, centralized, and utterly planned. It is communist. But what kind of communism does it exemplify? Certainly the very opposite of Marx's! Here there is an egalitarian redistribution of pooled resources. But private property is abolished? Yes, but the price to be paid for that abolition should make us stop and think: everything else is abolished along with it. Gone is all initiative, all creativity, everything that is specific and distinguishing, every possibility of introducing even the slightest change.

Please note: I am not defending private property by saying that its abolition is possible only in a totally conformist regime. What I am saying is that if all the utopists, without exception, have linked the abolition of private property with a complete police state and if they have turned society into a machine in which each individual is a tiny cog without any initiative of its own, the reason is that they have the highest possible esteem for private property. A utopia is never anything but the inverted image of the formula according to which private property is an inviolable, sacred right. Our utopists—all of them, all of them without a single exception—represent the most bourgeois kind of thinking.

As for work: up with work! Everyone must work, and do it under the complete control of an idealist hygiene, with even man's leisure being ordained, organized, and collectivized like everything else. Etienne Cabet, for example, decided that rationalized festivals should be obligatory.[7]

The most important thing of all is that nothing changes in utopia. Progress is repetition. Once society has reached this ideal state in which everything is smooth and aseptic and there are no problems and nothing happens, it is clear that any change would stimulate the need to adapt and thus cause uneasiness, a wrinkled brow, a question in the mind. But there must be no questions. Nothing must be allowed to happen.

In its frenzied pride, rationalist utopian thought exalts its own value, takes its position above history, and claims to sit in judgment on it. In this it is indeed "rationalist," for reason has in fact been dethroned and in its place sits ideology, mythology, the religion of reason. We are confronted here with a managerial mentality that takes itself for ultimate truth. "Its hope is not for a mankind redeemed or, as others would say, liberated, but for a micro-society that is completely planned and marvelously organized down to the least detail." Utopists are not interested in the real man or in the passionate flexibility of life, but only in rigid social mechanisms and the exercise of power. The utopist wants power so that he can organize man and society.

It is easy now to understand why utopian thinking has come into favor again in our society: utopianism is the ideology that corresponds perfectly to a technicized society. Technique is not yet everywhere successful, of course; it causes many a disturbance and disaster, and it is not clear how these can be avoided. But, just as the bourgeois who were terrified by messianic movements or uncontrolled forces, before which they felt helpless, responded by building a utopia in which everything would ultimately be mastered, controlled, and organized, so today, when technique is creating problems we cannot solve, these same bourgeois,[8] still panic-stricken and still unable to find a way out, make a great leap into utopia.

We must not let ourselves be fooled. Sometimes the description "utopia" is applied to Aldous Huxley's *Brave New World* or George Orwell's *Animal Farm,* but the word is then simply being misapplied. What these books offer is terrible models calculated to make us react against what is likely to happen; they do not present us with utopias. Utopian, on the contrary, is the revival of Marx's thought as utopian. The visions of many urbanologists (Yona Friedmann and others) and the current of thought represented by Ernst Bloch, Henri Lefebvre, and others show the specifically utopian characteristic of claiming to be the contrary of what they really are.[9] The bourgeois who constructed utopias used to put themselves forward as great revolutionaries when in fact they were utterly regressive in their thinking. So today the utopists claim to be crusaders against the technicization of society, when in fact they are allowing technique to move toward its fulfillment thanks to the breath of false oxygen offered by the utopianist evasion. Modern rationality takes shape in technique. Rationalism takes shape in utopias. When all is said and done, the technician and the utopist have the same goal in view.

This is why the utopists of our day think that at last they may be able to implement their program. Psychological methods may make it possible to impose complete conformity on everyone. Economic techniques may make possible a complete control of soil, environment, and the economy. It is now possible to have complete urbanization; the elimination of chance, including the chance involved in procreation (O blessed genetic

technology, now we can produce the ideal man!); a strict distribution of tasks and advantages; endless repetition, yet complete stability; a never-ending pedagogy, which means continuous information and therefore continuous formation.

But we should not forget the etymology of pedagogy and the
fact that it means keeping people permanently in the infantile
stage. Continuous formation, which is the great utopian ideology, implies that one never passes beyond the infantile stage
of life. But these objectives are identically those of technique.
How well met the utopist and the technician are! Utopia will
be the agent that carries the technical imperative into the souls
of men. It enables the technician to make men believe they are
at last achieving a society based on equality, because utopias
are egalitarian, and that dreaming is being restored to its right-
ful place, because utopias are always presented as embodying
the dreams of mankind. But here again we see the vicious
hypocrisy of utopianism in pretending to be the opposite of
what it really is, for utopias are by their very nature antidream.

Drawn by the street noises that make their way into his
study, the humanist looks out morosely on the traffic snarls,
and falls to thinking. He cannot endure the insults the road-
hogs sling at one another and the tense, anxious, worried,
tired appearance of the passersby.

He cannot endure such disorder and waste. Disorder is
everywhere. Motorcycles rev up with harrowing noises. Trucks
spill their exhaust unhindered to asphyxiate everyone around.
The traffic policemen jump in violently with insults in their
mouths and tickets in their hands; the drivers caught speeding
pull over in a double line, blocking the side streets. One stupid
and malicious fellow is determined to get through at any cost,
slips through wherever he thinks he sees enough room, weaves
from one lane to the other; he darts forward an inch, paying
no heed to those coming from the side; he barricades a passage where others might have got through, and hopelessly
blocks two or three lines of cars that are now utterly stymied.

The humanist dreams. He dreams of a city in which the
streets are wide and almost unbounded, all perfectly straight

with few access roads. It is a city in which drivers would move from their proper place only when strictly necessary, and would always be judging their personal likes and dislikes by the standard of the common good; they would be relaxed and happy, refusing all febrile activity and advancing only in unison, without any spirit of competition or unscrupulous ambition or even the possibility of getting ahead of others in any way. Gone is the spirit of power and domination, for lives are as perfectly straight as the streets. In addition, there would no longer be thirty-six different models of cars, with their varying beauty, speed, power, and size. Why should there be that kind of wasteful rivalry? No, there would be only one model, purely utilitarian and pragmatic, and all the cars would be the same color. Then no one could try to make others notice him, for from that desire a great deal of the trouble springs.

From the automobile the humanist inevitably passes on to all the other frivolous external signs: jewelry, garments lacking any rationale, and so forth. Why should anyone wear a tie? or blue jeans? It is perfectly clear that if you want men's behavior to be rational you must introduce rationality into all that forms the context of their lives. There can be no more giving in to traditions (these had their point at one time, of course, but they are meaningless today) or to fashions. Dress is nothing but frivolity and unreason. The humanist returns to his desk and meditates. His hand slides over the white paper and he sketches, somewhat inattentively, a figure wearing a dress that is perfectly satisfying in every detail. He observes, with pleasure, that, although not exercising his real talent, he always does well when he sketches from life. Then, too, why should women's dress differ from men's? There is no rational explanation. So, he goes on sketching, and his work . . . but there is no profit in just dreaming: dreaming is not good for body or soul. He now knows, however, the lines along which he must move.

The next day he goes back to his sketching, but now he turns to industry, in order to carry yesterday's work a step further. The noise is constant: How can anyone concentrate? Night begins to fall; suddenly, opposite his window, the harsh lights of a large store burst upon the darkness with a huge blinking sign, alternately white and red: three seconds white, three seconds red. Stupid, irrational blinking: objectionable, wasteful. He goes to the window: the whole street is a gaudy splash of neon signs. Whom do they expect to draw with these expensive fantasies? What is the value of this mad competitiveness, all this energy and intelligence wasted on advertising?

How simple it would be if in place of these countless stores there were but a single one, carefully organized according to strict divisions: a quiet, air-conditioned store in which the customer would find absolutely everything. No meaningless differences, no costly packaging, no multiplication of brands that stimulates "market research," which is nothing but a sheer waste of time, since when all is said and done all the competitors offer the same product under different names. A store, then, with perfectly straight aisles, and many quiet swift elevators; on each floor, everything you want, but in only one model. Think of all the time saved that is otherwise spent beating about the bush and discussing the merits of the various brands! Think of all the time the salespeople will save, since they will not have to demonstrate various models or try to convince the customer! You want an electric stove? Here it is: there is no other model. What a relief to everyone! No more showing off of brands and models; no need to play the comedy any longer.

The humanist has a vision. He sees the incredibly perfect city in which men will at last be freed from so many worries; in which hateful competition will be eliminated because everyone will be the same; in which everyone will contribute to the common task because there are no superiors and inferiors, and all will be in harmony with all else. The great objective is to remove the causes of conflict and all the waste.

But will it not be necessary to put a stop to public speeches and political addresses? The worried humanist asks himself the question, for he is certainly all in favor of freedom and has a horror of censorship. And yet, if that is the price that has to be paid . . . After all, what good are all the political addresses? The alternatives are sterile agitation, on the one side, and on the other, a concern for the well-being of the city, but a city so quiet and well organized that no one has any more claims to assert. Claims would only disturb and unsettle the marvelous order and balance we now have the technical means of achieving. Is this not all vain speculation, then? Political speeches add nothing, but only serve to let men voice their claims. In our marvelous city, however, no claims will be possible, because every need will be satisfied, gloriously satisfied.

Political speeches will be useless and strictly without purpose. Eliminating them, therefore, is really not an act of censorship at all, but something required by the nature of things. Futile divisions that would only upset good order are intolerable, and no one needs them. Inspired by this noble vision of brotherhood becoming at last a reality, the humanist goes a step further and asks whether poetry, too, will not have lost its justification. Regrets, aspirations, the flight into the vague, the uncertain, the unconscious—are not these marks of poetry a sign of disorder, dissatisfaction, and repressed desires? Is poetry not a futile and deceptive satisfaction that masks a deeper frustration? In our perfect city there will be no more frustration, no more conflict. There will be no more passions, and therefore poetry will cease to be of any use.

Music, too, must be eliminated, for it disturbs men and entices them into the darker regions of their being. The goal, however, is that everything should be clear; everything must be brought up to the surface of consciousness and submitted for judgment.

As the humanist watches, he sees young people entering the movie house; they jostle each other and laugh and argue, acting in countless imprudent and provoking ways—and yet they seem to be happy! That kind of happiness disturbs the humanist. How can people be happy amid such disorder and confusion? Ah, it is simply because they live so much of their lives at the unconscious level. We must fight against unconsciousness and the unconscious. Each individual must learn what he is made of; he must realize that his destiny is perfectly clear and marked out for him without the possibility of chance or surprise interfering. He must learn that he cannot offset a basic unhappiness with this comedy of laughter and jostling and that a reasonable, rational happiness can be permanently his instead of this factitious and really ridiculous "joy."

They must be taught, the humanist thinks as he returns to his desk. Yes, they must be taught. That is the only way, since it may take generations before man will be ready to enter the perfect city. Or perhaps we must ignore men and create the city without them, and then use a rigorous educational process to eliminate the irrationality that has been man's heritage?

With a sigh, the humanist goes back to work on designing the piping for a new heating system. Here, at least, he can find satisfaction, since all the conditions are objectively determined, and movement is regular and unhindered. The fluid is perfectly unified; no molecule claims to be special; everything is orderly. Here, at last, there is order.

Utopianism has been interpreted in many ways. The two most divergent interpretations are those of Georges Duveau, who sees in utopian thinking an approach to the adult, conscious, fully elaborated, voluntary stage of social life,[10] and of François Laplantine, who regards it as the expression of political schizophrenia. The two theses are not of equal validity, since the values that underlie each are opposed.

If pure rationality be the sole criterion, then utopian thinking is advanced and satisfying. But are these thinkers sure that it is not man himself (or what has till now been known under the name of "man") that they are abandoning? We always tend to put too much emphasis on the brain: man has won his victories because of his brain; as much as eighty percent of the brain's potential goes unused; and so on. If man is reduced to a brain, if he is no longer a body, if he is no longer to have any emotions, if he is to have no more relationships except those established by rational communication from which the whole realm of the emotional has been excluded, then a utopia is the model you want. But then you also want that frequently described future day in which man is separated from the body and his brain is attached directly to machines. On the other hand, if you want man preserved intact with all his complexity, then Laplantine's thesis is a strong one.

According to Laplantine, a utopia is a projection of the mother, for it expresses the desire for absolute stillness and the return to the maternal womb. "The traveler is taken under the wing of a mother who can satisfy all his needs and desires for food and growth." Laplantine's analysis is sure-sighted when it comes to the significance of the nutritional regimen, cleanliness, and hygiene. All these are signs of a return to the nursery. There is no longer any need of a father or a political authority who only cause trouble by interfering between the all-providing mother and her nurslings.

The individual, absorbed into these changeless structures of warm cosmic harmony finds himself alone as he tries to come to grips with all the maternal images; he sinks into a state of terrible submission, that is, into a psychotic state. . . . He wants nothing more than to keep his mother for himself alone. This partially explains the overwhelming hatred we find all utopists feeling toward strangers.

That is the first part of Laplantine's analysis. The second has to do with the abstractness of utopian schemes. The abstractness results from a rigorously rationalistic approach, but the approach would not be rigorously rationalistic were it not that the vital impulses, the unexpected, inventiveness, projects, fantasies, imagination, and communion had been excluded. The result is "a morbid susceptibility to the stereotyped and the abstract."

Laplantine draws the parallel between schizophrenia and utopia. The parallel depends on "a structural homology that is at the basis both of utopia as a totalitarian political system, and of the utopian consciousness of the citizens who live under such a system." There are several specific points of comparison. The first is this: utopia is marked by a desire to be freed once and for all from the burden of having to make decisions, and by the members' joyous acceptance of a total dependence, in which they find their happiness and which they consider to be freedom. But "we know how difficult it is for the schizophrenic to make decisions and how stubbornly he seeks dependence at any price and unquestioning submission to the orders of the institution."

The second point of comparison seems to me to be obvious. Utopia, we have repeatedly said, is not an intelligent invention; it is, rather, a betrayal of reason by rationalism, which is blind because it is incapable of accepting reality as norm and measure. Rationalism is "a monstrous excrescence of reason." The schizophrenic likewise locks himself up within himself and becomes unresponsive to the outside world; experience has no influence on him, and he thus loses all real relationship to life.

Laplantine shows sound judgment when he demonstrates that utopia is not simply a theoretical model of a distant reality. On the contrary, with the help of technical equipment we are in a position to make utopia an almost complete reality; more than that, by reasons of techniques that form a system we are actually moving toward utopia. Laplantine finds in the behavior of city dwellers numerous schizophrenic traits that result from the technical systematization just mentioned:

> The real schizoid inappetency, rigidity, and fixated, catatonic behavior we see today in our large cities is a clinical fact. . . . day by day, in our least gesture and in our innermost attitudes, we are being taken over by models which I could equally well describe as utopian or as technophrenic . . . The coldness, the lack of affectivity, the inability to engage deeply and in a truly personal way in human relationships . . . The obsession with symmetry, plan, program, calculation, and all forms of insurance.

All these tendencies, which would justify a diagnosis of mental illness, are signs that the desire for utopia is present in our midst.

A final point of comparison is this. We see a tendency to imprison the self in an immobile, sociocentric existence that goes to considerable lengths in striving for a morbidly artificial balance and that has for a corollary a denial of time and the event. It is a tendency that is evidently characteristic of utopias. But it is at the same time characteristic of schizophrenia with its well-known inability to relate to the temporal process. The schizophrenic is anxious lest something unforeseen occur in his life. "It is this typically psychotic negation of life's superabundance and of movement and history that the creator of a utopia exalts as a value."

In conclusion, Laplantine offers these two striking formulations. On the one hand, the "schizo-utopian" structure leads to a narrowing of vision that consists in reducing the polyphonic ambivalence of symbols to the univocal monovalence of signs. On the other hand, utopian thought is marked by a frantic pursuit of dualism and a hatred of everything that is dialectical. Everything in utopia is divided into contraries, and utopian thinking bids us choose good vs. evil, day vs. night, order vs. incoherence, effectiveness vs. distraction, the straight line vs. the curved line, the cerebral vs. the spontaneous, the planned vs. the vital, and space vs. time. The universe is clearly divided in two, and we are to choose the one side and reject the other. That is the attitude a schizophrenic takes, but it also typifies the very opposite of reason.

Reason is not an iron collar set on the neck of reality, nor does it divide reality into irreconcilable opposites. On the contrary, it relates man to reality so as to situate him within it and to make "the real" something he can understand and live with. I use the word "understand" to mean an effective comprehension, not abstract intellection, still less an analytic fragmentation. Reason, as developed in the West, has indeed had an element of control, but it is a control measured by reason itself, and has not meant the kind of exclusiveness and sclerosis associated with utopian thinking.

The passage to utopia by way of rationalism shows quite clearly the process by which the West has betrayed reason, which is to say the process by which reason has betrayed itself. Each discovery and each advance the West made was necessarily accompanied by the emergence of a contradiction and by openness to some new adventure. Reason remained reason only to the extent that man and the universe were basically nonrational and the vital powers continued to be limitlessly greater than all the controls reason sought to exercise. Reason built its order and regularity on a subconscious, which it sought to bring to light, understand, and control, but which made itself felt ever anew with consuming, devastating power. Reason proved a marvelous instrument for tirelessly reweaving the fine, exactly patterned, organizing spider's web that is constantly rent asunder by the cyclonic passage of a huge wandering bee.

But reason also possesses the means of power, and this led to the moment of choice, when a choice was made without deciding and choosing, by a kind of mischance in programming. Reason ceased to be itself and became simply the center of a vast machinery that ceased to obey it. The logic of means, the logic of the will to use means tore reason from its native soil, for logic is reason stood on its head.

This brings us to the most complicated problem in the whole process of betrayal: I mean the combination of Apollo and Dionysus, the head of Apollo set on the body of Dionysus. To put it in other words: science and technique, which has originally been an expression of reason, were no longer at its service and under its control so that they preserved their original legitimacy, but were now in the service of insanity, irrationality, and extremism. I am always astounded when I hear people nowadays calling for a return to instinct, the irrational, madness, as though we did not already have the most remarkable example of these qualities in the higher technicians or in Hitler, the prototype of them all.

I have the feeling that our brilliant intellectuals are unfortunately looking only for the most simplified and obvious expressions of madness; the gesticulations of an Artaud, for example. Despite their claims, they have not realized that the decisions of the politicians and technicians belong to a much more subtle and advanced order of madness—and a much more fearful one, since these men are deciding on reality and have the means to implement their decisions. In the movie *Zabriskie Point*, the youths make the irrational, mad decision to blow up the capitalist's home. Quite unintentionally, however, the director makes it clear how very much the adult world is also the expression of a madness: the very same madness as has seized the young, although it manifests itself differently. In both cases the madness of power, domination, destruction of others is at work.

Madness and spontaneity, then, are by no means an answer to the technicians. The West has betrayed itself because its reason has come to be dominated by hybris, without on that account becoming any less effective. Reason no longer exists, but what it has produced is still there. The means it has brought into existence are now in the hands of the mad, bewitching god who concentrates on making insane decisions and implementing them at the cost of endless destruction. (I certainly include the technological luxury and comfort of modern bathroom facilities as part of this destruction.)

But how could such an unnatural alliance have come about? How could reason have thus foundered? How could it have been enslaved? In my opinion, a curse attached to the progress of reason from the very beginning, and reason could not bear up under the contradictions it had itself engendered. It had to resolve them all, and in a reasoned, reasonable world contradictions became a scandalous and unacceptable burden. The stubborn effort of western thought to eliminate contradictions has been one of the great things about the whole western adventure. The West has been determined to reduce everything to unity, to pull everything together into a coherent whole, to leave nothing unexplained, to tolerate no circle of outer darkness, to reject the idea that there was anything, however hidden, which the mind could not bring into the light.

Far more than of the scientists and philosophers (though they all shared the same determination and orientation), I am thinking of the theologians and the incredible course of western theology. On the one hand, western theology has refused to accept any divergence, discontinuity, or distance between God and man, and has done everything in its power to reduce one of these two terms to the other. On the other hand, it has had a horror of mysteries and has spent centuries exploring the being of God, "explaining" the Trinity, and shedding light on the mysteries; in the process, it has shown a relentless eagerness that would have been more profitably devoted to some less foolish project.

This determination to eliminate contradictions and to bring all secrets to light has produced two major consequences.

First, we excluded and eliminated whatever would surely lead to a contradiction. The passion for unity simply annihilated whatever continued to resist assimilation or gave rise to new questions. We find this obsession with unity manifesting itself at the national level and even on the world scale. The good people who get excited because "two-thirds of mankind is dying of hunger"[11] and who call for unlimited aid from the "rich nations" (this is something I am for, if it is properly understood), express *only*—I emphasize the word "only"—the passion for world unity. They do so because the world is evidently one and undivided (just as in the Middle Ages it was evident that the church was one) and we who make up the world must necessarily share each other's lot. (This is just one small example.)

The second and more basic consequence of this search for unity at any price was to make a single whole out of the insane and the reasonable: the insane policies of monarchs and the managerial skills of administrators, the mad magic of the activists and the scientific reason of the researchers, the Ship of Fools and the urban order. There was a complete contradiction here. Reason could not tolerate the disordered grimaces of madness, and yet with its well-known efficiency the West managed to do just that! Now madness is enthroned at the very heart of western efficiency, in the geometry course, in science itself, and it is this marvelous combination that provides utopia as its splendid proof.

To put it a bit differently: all the undertakings of western reason are now falsified and perverted by the madness that has laid hold of reason. The passion for clarity and unity has caused us to reject that which was the West's great source of strength and originality (in the literal sense: that which gave rise to the West), namely, not the division of reality into two irreconcilable worlds, but the process of dialectical interplay between irreducibly hostile forces that thereby rendered each other fruitful: to wit, controlling reason and wild passion. In the confusion, however, reason, along with all the power it had accumulated, has come to be simply a horse for a mad rider.

The West has denied itself by not making contradiction part

of its own movement; for example, the contradiction between reason and self-consciousness (with the latter necessarily leading man to admit that the only reasonable self-consciousness involved the transcending of reason). More important still, the West rejected the contradiction between Eros and Agape. Today, Agape is bent on being absorbed into the exaltation of Eros.

Reason has been betrayed, and we now have nothing more to fall back on that would enable us to resume our journey. All reasonable discourse, every discovery, every proclamation is either powerless or wears the yoke of hybris. Only the mad exercise of power, whether on the right or on the left, whether among philosophers or among scientists, wins public favor and the approval of one's peers. No one is interested now in reasonable thinking or basic propositions, whereas everyone goes wild about the absurd, the mad, the passionate, the spontaneous in literature and in philosophy; everyone is eager for the plunge into the depths of the unconscious or the occult, provided it is matched by the organizing power of technique. The reverse is also true: technique contains within itself, indeed it is itself, the madness of power or hybris, and consequently can serve only such thinking as manifests the same characteristics. We need not claim that technique was made to serve Stalin's madness; but we may indeed say that this man's utter madness corresponded perfectly to the madness inherent in technique, and that this is why he could make use of it. There is a difference only of degree and completeness, not of kind, between Stalin's madness and that of a highway engineer who uses his absolute power to make a road system that defies all reasonable reason.

Such, then, is the betrayal of reason and history.

2 *The Betrayal of the Individual: The Executioner*

When it became necessary for the first time, back at the dawn of history, for men to kill a member of their own clan, great terror fell upon them all at their inexpiable crime. They were being forced to tear out a piece of their own flesh and to destroy spiritual powers; the man who slew his brother was laying sacrilegious hands on the mysterious balance prevailing between good and evil.

The first great step, therefore, was somehow to evade the responsibility. This was done by regarding the guilty person as slain not by men but by the gods, as handed over to the gods for punishment. He might be set adrift in a boat with his hands and feet tied; he might be immured in a cave with a minimum of food, as a guilty vestal virgin later would be; he might be driven out into the desert, unarmed, with a flask of water, as a scapegoat loaded down with the sins of the people.

In that view of the world, a man did not kill his fellow clansman; he simply handed him over to the offended gods, and no one knew what went on in that encounter of criminal and divinity. In some mysterious way, vengeance was taken, and the order that had been disturbed was restored; the whole business was now a private matter between the guilty person and the divine powers. It would be an oversimplification, therefore, to say that the vestal virgin was killed by being entombed. Society refused any responsibility for her death, and it was not being hypocritical. The guilty party's death was a judgment by the god, and it was not for man to act as the god's substitute; in playing the part he did, man acted not as an executioner but as a priest and a magus, for no mere human being had the right to intervene in the solemn encounter of the criminal and the god. As for ourselves, we may no longer believe in the same divinities, but we do maintain that man's encounter with death is a solemn moment, and indeed the uniquely decisive moment of his life. It is good that at this moment man should be alone, for he really is alone, and that, free of ceremonies, false consolations, and false terrors, and free especially of the false presences and the lies, he should be for a moment face to face with his destiny.

Times changed. Transgressions multiplied and the social body closed ranks to defend itself. The balancing of crime and punishment began to seem a balance that society and men must maintain. Man came to think of himself as delegated by the gods in important matters, and he accepted his responsibility. He distinguished between ritual slaying and slaying for revenge; between offenses against the divinity and offenses against the clan, the group, and the family (though not as yet against the individual); and between kinds of penalty. He agreed to act as substitute for the divinities of the lower world in inflicting death; thus, though the gods were still called upon to pass judgment by way of the ordeal, it was man who now decided to carry out the judgment.

The judgment and the penalty were now seen as distinct, whereas previously they had been regarded as a single decision, with men inferring guilt from the fact that the penalty had been inflicted. Now the penalty was the mechanical execution of the judgment of guilt. It had to be mechanical: there could be no escape from it, no forgetfulness or pardon. Once the gods had pronounced the guilty verdict, man carried out the sentence, for he had no one else to depend on in seeing that the effect automatically followed from the cause.

Thus the executioner appeared on the scene: the man garbed in red so that the victim's blood might not be visible, but also because red was the color of hell; the man who was masked so that the people, who hated him, might not be able to recognize him, but also because the face of the man who kills without a personal motive becomes intolerable, and because the man whose face is exposed to the fires of the sacred cannot turn that face, unmasked, to men. The executioner was the object of fear and detestation, and his eyes bore the look of one who had done the unforgivable. He lived alone and outside the village, for what woman would be willing to share his covenant with hell? The executioner was also a sorcerer, because he destroyed life, and the village could not accept his shame and uncleanness.

The executioner was no less accursed than the victim who was handed over to him. He was brother to the condemned man whom he slew, because the entire community shifted its sins onto the shoulders of both. Contact with him rendered others unclean, and the sight of him inspired fear.

At this stage, the whole business was still aureoled with

mystery. The executioner did his work in darkness, and the dungeons of the Inquisition, like the execution chamber of the Châtelet,[12] was underground, down where the rough-hewn rock walls seeped water, and the air was filled with smoke from resin-soaked torches. The people did not know what went on there. All was secret, and only one man—not the priest, but the executioner— stood between the condemned man and the god. Down there, brother indeed slew brother; both were iniquitous, both criminals. Meanwhile, up above, the people of the town went about with the bad conscience that prevented them from looking at the executioner as he emerged through the barred gate.

Soon, however, men began to cultivate more correct feelings in this area. No longer did the god condemn, but the state —and who could believe that the state might be unjust or act without authority? No, it was necessary to relieve man of his bad conscience, which seemed to say that his justice was no justice at all. Man was part of the state, and if the state was just, then man should regard himself as likewise justified. If the need to kill arose, then it was good to kill at the command of the state.

The executioner was now no longer connected with the supernal or infernal powers; he was simply an instrument of the state, carrying out not divine decrees but the just judgment of the authorities. There was nothing mysterious about it now. At the same time, however, it was only right that the punishment should inspire a salutary fear, since this would prevent new crimes; fear of the sacred was to be replaced by fear of the police. The punishment had therefore to be dreadful and public, so as to make a deep impression on the community; it had to touch the imagination rather than the religious sense. Consequently, the scaffold was built at the center of the larger town. An execution became a solemn ceremony, a festive occasion with the people milling around, frightened yet experiencing the sensual pleasure the horrible can arouse, and with the state looking on from the balcony at the evidence of its power.

The role of the executioner had changed. He was now not a mediator but simply an agent, not a sorcerer but a functionary; his actions were no longer mysterious and sacred, but public and dramatic. He was no longer tarred with the same brush as his victim, but stood on the other side of a barrier: he now represented justice and was executor of the state in its loftiest role as arbiter of life and death.

The people, however, were not so easily convinced. This man continued to be for them the focus of certain spiritual beliefs, and they could not look on his face without a feeling of horror. For the people retained an innate respect for human life, and knew quite well that doing the killing in the light of day changed nothing: it was still a dark deed. The executioner might, therefore, no longer be accursed, but he remained a pariah. He was unlike anyone else, he was brother to no one, and the death he dealt out on orders surrounded him with a solitude no one dared enter. Formerly, each member of the community had felt bound to the executioner by his own bad conscience, for the executioner, though living apart from the community, was nonetheless a member of it and carried its sins on his shoulder; unlike the priest, he was detested, since he was indispensable to the community and yet a cause of shame to it as well; no one could look into his face without seeing in it a reflection of his own guilt, and therefore all chose to ignore him and pass him by. Now that the executioner had become an agent of the state, he was simply absent from among the people. He no longer bore the sins of the people but performed a function for the state and, having become a stranger to his victim, he became a stranger to society as well.

Though disavowed by both the living and the dead, the executioner still exercised a strong personal attraction. His ill-repute might be intensified when it took seven blows of the ax to dispatch Marie Antoinette, but he could also win admiration if he were a virtuoso with the sword. But then came the machine. Whether it employed rope or iron, a machine was surer, more capable, more unfailing than the hand. The part played by the executioner became less extensive, and at the same time his appearance and position changed.

Civilization now pushed its way into all the mire and slime, and brought hygiene with it. It was regarded as unhealthy to expose the populace to such spectacles. Besides, the fear of punishment did not become any less when the punishment was hidden. In fact, bringing the tortured man before crowds often turned him into an object of public sympathy, whereas the blood of martyrs does not become the seed of confessors if the simple are not allowed to attend the ceremony. The heroism of condemned men can change the course of history, and the state only loses prestige when its enemies face death in the presence of all. Far better, then, to make the whole business much less dramatic. The gallows are therefore erected in a courtyard; the midday sun no longer shines on justice at its work, for the cold dawn sees the victim out.

The executioner no longer dresses in red; little if any blood is shed now, and reason has proved that demons do not exist. Nor is the executioner masked, since the only persons present are the judge, the lawyer, and the priest—all of them accomplices in the one act and possessing powers that make them brothers to the executioner. They can all look at one another without laughing. The executioner, in addition, is no longer a public figure; his name is known indeed, and his face by those who have seen him, but these people do not point the finger at him.

The executioner lives in the city; he is a citizen, a voter, father of a family, and, all in all, a decent fellow. His face is a reassuring one, for he is a democrat; besides, we know that under a liberal and free-thinking republic death itself is no longer fearful. The executioner now carries out a public function; he is a civil servant. Could anything be more reassuring or less frightening than that? Why, the man has a country cottage and grows roses there! In addition, he really has little to do with the inflicting of death: all he does is press a button, and the button may even be in another room. The blade falls, the trapdoor opens, the spark crosses the gap—and death goes with it. But who summoned death? The executioner is now only one personage in the drama; he is even forgotten amid the parade of the high and mighty. His action has become as respectable as his person and his function.

And yet the executioner is a real person. In any instance,

there is only one executioner. His action is ordered according to ceremony and controlled by the authorities. The whole of society is present when he carries out his task; everyone knows how the entire human community is still fascinated by the finger that pushes this special button. People may talk about it only to themselves, but somehow the secret is faithfully passed on, and those who are in on it still feel the cold sweat on their brow, as did the earliest primitives before them.

Soon, however, there will be no more secret horror. "Life has spun on its furious heel,"[13] and the world is now simplistically divided into the good people and the bad people. He who is unjust in the eyes of the state no longer has the right to live. He is punished not for a positive, carefully delimited crime, but because he does not fit into the precise, delimited framework of justice. Because he does not agree with the rest of us, he is evil. He does not simply do evil, he incarnates it.

If a person does evil, we may hope to set him straight by modern methods. But what can be done with the person who incarnates evil? There is no alternative but for him to disappear, so that the evil may disappear with him. He will descend the iron staircase with its wrought-iron steps and treacherous pitch. The spiraling movement brings him to a windowless room with clean, unadorned cement walls, lit harshly by a cold electric light that is as luminous as the truth and as straightforward as the distinction between good and evil. In this room there are no shadows, for there is nothing to hide, and if the room is underground, that is solely to make the technical side of things easier.

There is no furniture in the room, since there is nothing to be done there, and besides, furniture is a sign of evolution. But evolution stops here: there is only a drain-channel running around the cement floor and emptying into the main outlet. The man looks around at what might well be a room in a clinic, and as he does, a report behind him announces that the job is done. There is no time any more for ceremonial or supervision in connection with executions; evil is now incarnate in too many forms, and we must hurry and get rid of it in the simplest and easiest way we can. There is not even an official executioner now; the person who pulls the trigger is only someone from the crowd. There are many who can play the role; many, perhaps, who want to do it, for it is an honor, a role that contributes to the safety and well-being of the community.

"Play the role"? But it really is not a role any more. It is simply part of life, and the executioner is probably anonymous. No one in the crowd is likely to recognize him. As at the dawn of history, he is unknown; but it is no longer a mask that renders him anonymous, only the crowd itself. He is anonymous because he melts into the mass of men, whereas in olden times he was anonymous because he was cut off by his hood. Anyone in the group can be or become the executioner, if he is worthy of this supreme service. And if he be in fact unknown, everyone honors him like the unknown soldier, for he is part of the communion of the just.

How far we have come from the primitive darkness in which the executioner was linked to the community by bad conscience and a sense of having violated the sacred, as well as in the desperate effort to restore balance and justice (an effort that certainly required victims)! Now we are all bound together by a good conscience and by the certainty that we require no pardon, since an execution is simply a hygienic act. Yet mystery remains, and in this respect, as in the practice of executing men underground, we are at one with the primitive ages. But the mystery is no longer a mystery of iniquity: it is a mystery of goodness. For, by his action, the executioner reaches the heights of goodness and justice to which the collectivity may aspire. This is all the more true to the extent that he acts without either sadistic anger or compassion. When a man harvests grain in order to feed his family, does he think of the life that quivers in the plants he is cutting down? The executioner is in a similar position: for him the victim has become a thing—and that is the other side of the mystery.

The evil the collectivity sees and uncovers in the wrongdoer turns the latter into a neutral object. The Middle Ages brought to light the evil lurking in sorcerers, and then burned them at the stake in order to assure their eternal salvation. Today, social hygiene has eliminated the individual as one who can be saved or lost. What he was previously and what he may become subsequently matter little; the guilt the state sees in him cancels him out even before his death. As machine technology removes the human dimension from the act of execution, so do organizational techniques make the act an act of the collectivity, and psychological techniques make it a normal part of life.

"There is no mystery about the executioner," said reason, fifty years ago. "There is still a mystery," says our age, "but a splendid and encouraging mystery." For all the executioner does now is carry out a "physical liquidation." Are the words mere hypocrisy, or a euphemism tossed up by our technical civilization? No, they imply, and with justice, that the condemned person is already dead: he has placed himself outside of the truth and of justice, and by that very fact has ceased to exist; he no longer has any personal, spiritual life; he is merely a relic, a set of physical organs that continues to exist but has no reason for doing so. The executioner merely restores proper order; death comes from his hand in response to a death earlier inflicted. And in his new role, which is a sign of new worlds opening before us, the cold bright light of the execution chamber makes him look like an archangel.

Yet, even when we had reached this point, there was further progress still to be made. This object which was only seemingly alive—the condemned man who was already dead—could still be of service. In a world where utility is the universal law, how could such a source of wealth for society be neglected? Rational methods had stripped the condemned man of his tragic relationship with death; now they went a step further and shifted him over into the category of the useful. This individual is no longer another person; the veil of personality has been removed. He is now nothing but a zombie—but everything must be used.

There was a time when we were horrified to learn that soap and fabric were made out of the corpses in the concentration camps. But why were we horrified? After all, it was a simple piece of technology. And those, Christian theologians among them, who said the young survivors of the airplane wreck in the Andean Cordillera were right to have eaten the bodies of their companions, have thereby justified what was done in the concentration camps. Eat a corpse to save your own life? After all, why not? The free-thinkers have shown us that the condemnation of cannibalism was simply a survival of absurd taboos. How can the body be something sacred?

Yes, yes, of course. But then why not use human bodies to make preserves if society needs them for its survival? We are already enlightened by the Green Sun.[14] And how can we fail to believe that the overall needs of society are infinitely more urgent, decisive, justifying, and objective than the empty stomach of the man who, after a bit of resistance, eats his neighbor's arm? In this case there is no resistance, because the necessity is collective. Never has society been in a better position over against the individual. Never has society been so exalted, and never has it so utterly denied the individual.

Even this service rendered by the man already dead is not enough. After all, the individual belongs body and soul to his society. Even his soul? Of course! How, then, can we let it depart before it has completely emptied itself, before it has been wrung out and made to yield its full contents? The person who will shortly be executed may still have some secret he ought to yield up, some secret that would disappear when his mouth is forever shut. Yet no secret should remain secret. The living person should be spied on, filmed, photographed in his innermost recesses, heard by a thousand ears, known in every least detail of his behavior, and filed away in the great electronic brain.

But suppose something is still hidden there? Some tiny detail society needs, that may be lost? Then use torture. The man must speak. He must give voice to what he himself perhaps no longer knows, something buried so deep that no psychoanalyst could bring it to light. Torture can get at it. The hypothetical relation, which is as important as the real; the sigh suppressed; the aspiration kept hidden: society must have knowledge of them all. Everything must be known so that everything may be calculated and the calculation may be correct. But is torture just another name for repression? Non-sense! We have got beyond that sort of thing. Is it sadism? The question shows a radical misunderstanding, but one in which we find reassurance, for we can parallel it to the terrible wickedness of a Massu, that is, of an individual.[15] But, in this business, there are no individuals on either side!

Torture is something scientific, the torturer is a technician, and the victim is a fragment of society that must utter its confession. Torture as practiced by our ancestors? Torture in the Middle Ages? These have nothing in common with torture as used today. In ages past, torture was originally a form of sacrifice to the gods, before whom all felt the same terror. Later on, it was a way of inquiring into the destiny and sins of a person, the sins being known in all their specificity, particularity, and individuality for having been confessed under torture.

In all those instances, the victim was an individual and acknowledged as such. We have turned the clock back on that sort of undisciplined progress. The fact that society is abstract and technique neutral enables us to avoid embarrassing questions. Yet who speaks out in indignation? The purveyors of good conscience and the signers of protests are ready to close their eyes to tortures inflicted on the enemies of their cause; of course, since these enemies no longer exist as human beings. The tiger cages are an utter disgrace; but the subtle tortures of the Cultural Revolution? a mere unimportant detail! And if we find ourselves pushed back from position after position because the evidence is undeniable, well then, we must save the republic—or democracy, or socialism, or the revolution—must we not? In every instance, society comes first.

The torture that is commonplace today is not the result of chance or of a regression to barbarian times or of a particular regime or of an accidental turn down the wrong road. It is the strictly logical consequence of this denial of the individual, in which the West has denied itself, body and soul, to the profit of the collectivity, of objectivity, of technique. For, even if there be no more soul, there is still this final service the condemned man must render to society: he must survive, for the social good, in the form of the tiny secret he yielded up before being swallowed by death.

3 The Betrayal of Love and Freedom: The Grand Inquisitor

Who really loves man? That is the great question our age is anxiously asking amid all the immense promises and even amid all the marvelous accomplishments, the quasi-miracles that are within reach of our hand. But is it really a question? No, for in our hearts we know that the die is already cast and the answer already given and accepted. Who can really and truly claim to love man, but the one who meets his needs, or, more accurately, assuages his hungers? Nothing new about that. Of course not: "bread and circuses"! On the other hand, we must recognize that the Caesars did not manage to guarantee bread for the peoples of the empire. The great novelty of our century, and the thing that enables us to answer the opening question with such confidence, is that we now have all the means of guaranteeing nourishment and of assuaging every hunger.

Man loves the person who feeds him—and, even more, the person who *can* feed him. We can immediately find confirmation in the spiritual realm: Does not St. Paul say that good will is meaningful, not in itself, but because of what it possesses? Yes, we have become so demanding that we ask for tangible proofs. No more concessions in this respect: if you provide real and lasting nourishment, you are a benefactor of mankind. Of course, when we speak of "food," we use the term figuratively, for everyone knows that today "daily bread" means an automobile, a television set, and caviar for everybody. It is called "raising the standard of living." Here we have a tangible kind of love that does not deceive; a love that requires of those who exercise it great abnegation, patient research, and prudent calculation, but also an outpouring of heartfelt sentiment. Raise the standard of living; everything else is verbiage: words, words, words.

After all, we know full well today how empty language is, and what fools we were to believe it had any substance. Words are mere conventions that provide an abode for images created to no purpose by the various cultures; they say nothing, they transmit nothing. If at some special moment we have the feeling that a word has indeed passed from one person to another, such a feeling must be subjected to careful analysis. When it is put through the rolling-mill, only a few wretched shreds emerge.

Do you dare claim, then, that language, which is so wanting, can be a valid witness to love for man? a witness and an instrument of that kind of love? Do you still not understand what hypocrisy is? We can appeal once again to the spiritual realm for confirmation: Did not Jesus condemn those who talk but fail to act? Silence is today the only acceptable accompaniment of action. Why? Because there is no such thing as communication; the word impinges on the ear and fades into indistinctness; the hand may touch another hand, but not another being. What is left, then? Only to give bread to the hungry. We do not claim to communicate anything thereby, but at least we do not lie and pretend that our words carry love across the gap. We do not offer others the empty food of our dreams and thoughts. We have got rid of fine sentiments. We know now that we live in a vast solitude, and that the only relations between men are those of the wolf pack. But I am digressing; we were speaking of love.

Let me summarize: language is an illusion; the only thing that makes me a man is to bear human witness to the other by helping him. Really? Perhaps it is not an accident that the absence of communication and the emptiness of language have been discovered in the century in which consumer goods have multiplied. Shall I say that, now that his hands are full, man no longer needs factitious consolation from empty words that lulled him and made him forget his hunger? Or shall I, rather, say that a full belly has no ears with which to hear? "Israel, you have grown fat, and you no longer hear the word of your God," said the prophet.

In any case, the situation is what it is. Those who love man

are clear about their duty: they must feed him. Those who rule
men realize that they will not remain long in power if they do
not apply every technical means to raising the living standard.
In fact, we are now witnessing a rather marvelous union of
roles: those who love man are becoming his rulers, and those
who rule him are the ones who love him most.

This is indeed the century of the highest bid, a bid infinitely
more awe-inspiring than the campaign promises broadcast by
the second-rate politicians: "I will build you a dam," "I will
build you a television station," "I will have a hundred shiploads of wheat brought in," "And I ten thousand technicians."
We know now that the Grand Inquisitor is not an evil man.[16]
On the contrary, he alone truly loves man. All who have
preceded him have simply made game of man. Look at the
Grand Inquisitor building roads and factories and houses. Listen to him as he works out his complicated systems in order
at last to distribute to all, in the proper way, the goods produced by his clever machinery. He has no choice now but to
love man; he is forced to do so by the swelling torrent of
potentialities at his disposal. He is faced with a necessity, not
a choice.

How consoling that is to us! At last we are assured that this
true love of man will be an effective reality. Henceforth we
shall no longer have to walk the dark avenues of power or be
subject to the tortuous plans of men. Everything is now out in
the open and follows the clear light of a finished design. Just
think: there was a time when men could invoke "reason of
state"! How terribly simplistic—as though the state possessed
reason! And all that such an appeal led to was madness and
slaughter!

Now we know that there is a higher and fully legitimate
reason. What motivates the state is the good of man, and we
have now reached the stage of certainties that can be effectively implemented. We know that the overseer of the whole
operation is a man of total abnegation. But if he toils so pain-
fully, it is to spare men every possible difficulty; and if each
engineer applies his method with passionate fervor, if each
politician commits himself to the development and maturation

of man, all do so not for their own sake but for the sake of all.

I am aware, of course, that there are still black sheep around: politicians looking for personal success and learned men thirsty for power. We have passed judgment on such, however, and many of them have already been hanged. In any case, they are judged at the tribunal of history. For we no longer lack criteria with which to evaluate the politicians and the scholars; we are no longer interested in the agitated debates by jurists and theologians on justice and love. We know now perfectly well who really loves man, for it is something we can put to the test every day; it is no longer a matter of opinion or of the party you follow (all that sort of thing is outmoded now, passé). If the end is the same for everyone, then the means cannot really differ. Behind the outward appearances of regimes and doctrines (which are only verbiage anyway) we have all experienced man's coming of age, and no one will ever again make us revert to the past. Our age has turned us into individuals: grownup, well groomed, well fed, and independent; by that very fact we know that the only true humanist is the Grand Inquisitor.

Let us turn now to more important matters. For the system follows a kind of logic that is calculated both to disquiet and to satisfy us. The person who lives in hunger and terror cannot be—without any qualification, *cannot* be—a human being. Now, for the first time, man is receiving sufficient food and security from someone other than a very unmerciful Nature or a hypothetical divinity: he is receiving them from man. Man is secure, and because he has food in abundance, everything else is added: intelligence and goodness; a sense of beauty and a desire for justice.

From now on, because he is no longer preoccupied with the search for necessities of life, he can devote himself to what is superfluous: the arts and morality (these, as everyone knows, are the normal superfluities of those who are well provided for, as the nineteenth-century bourgeoisie made clear). But, you may say, that is no great discovery. We have always known, after all, that *primum est vivere:* staying alive is the first and most important thing. Well, I tell you, you have not understood what I have been saying. What we are talking about here is not situated at such a low level of thought as that. On the contrary: what strikes me when I contemplate the architectural detail of the new world that is now being born before our eyes is the utter intelligence of the Grand Inquisitor. He is so intelligent that he knows other intelligent men will regard him as vulgar, materialistic, and superficial—but that is part of his abnegation.

The Grand Inquisitor has accurately understood the deeper reality of things and men. He has fully grasped the spiritual ideals—true or false—that obsess men, and the debates—serious or frivolous—with which we occupy ourselves. He has grasped it all fully, and knows he cannot hope to eliminate the ideals or the debates. He knows that completely to satisfy every need of man would still not make man stop rebelling. It was not hunger, after all, that made Cain stoop and pick up the stone (the Inquisitor knows that perfectly well). How unstable the power of the ruler who sends his shiploads of grain to feed a starving people! How empty the hopes of the man in authority who thinks there will be no trouble because the salaries keep going up steadily! Have these people not learned that throughout history rebellions have broken out precisely when men are no longer crushed, hungry, and deprived of the necessities of life? That is when they look for "freedom." Of course! That is what we have been saying! Anyone who raises the living standard soon learns this everyday lesson. He knows how untenable his position is in the long run, and that as a distributor of goods there is one he cannot afford to overlook.

The Grand Inquisitor is a man of keen discernment, whether through study and the patient analysis of statistics or through profound intuition. He knows that without religion—some form of religion—his power is always unstable, always threatened. The man whose belly is full cannot live without also having something to adore. It may be the state, science, technique, race, communism, blackness, history, culture; it may be any god off the shelf, whatever will distract him for a day. The important thing is that there be a religion with its dogmas and rituals; the higher the religion, of course, the better.

Whatever be his own opinions and political or philosophical options, the Grand Inquisitor knows that power cannot afford to neglect the spiritual. The spiritual is a need of man and must be satisfied. Man must be given reasons for self-dedication, obedience, work; quite simply, he must be given a reason for living, since without such a reason material things lose their savor and their luster. The situation of man is unstable, as those in authority today know only too well. It is part of authority's mission to complete in the spiritual realm what was begun in the temporal. The spirituality must, however, be tidy and regulated; it must be geared accurately to satisfying man's restlessness and pride, and not be any longer the kind of spirituality that those in power know to be empty and without substance. The Grand Inquisitor himself is, of course, inevitably a skeptic. Not in any Machiavellian way, as though he were simply pretending to seek the good of the people; no, he really loves men. But does love not require that he give them what they need, even if it is in fact a lie and an illusion?

Power is skeptical, and rightly so. Should we expect it to involve itself in spiritual undertakings that would rob it of its power to calculate coolly and to preserve a necessary distance from all situations? At the same time, however, power cannot last if man does not adore it. To achieve this goal and to acquire the monumental quality, the changeless marble front, in which men can find satisfaction, everything must serve it. Nor is such an outlook the fruit of empty utilitarianism.

Everything must, of course, be useful. This statement marks the great progress made by our society today; for, a century ago, it thought it could divide all goods into useful goods and futile goods. Today, however, a deeper understanding of the human heart has taught us that nothing which man has created in the course of his history is really futile. Everything has been fashioned to serve him: even what does not exist; even what is only a dream, pursuing a phantom life in the depths of the obsessed heart. Everything must be of service, because nothing has ever been made without some purpose, and if man today can walk in triumph along the road of longer life expectancy, it is because for the profit of mankind the fatherly, self-sacrificing Grand Inquisitor has made such careful use of everything.

If the Grand Inquisitor retains his power, he does so not for selfish reasons but because he knows that only if his power grows can man live. If the Inquisitor makes use of religion, he does not do so like a bitter, ironic illusionist; rather, he sacrifices his own clear-eyed convictions to the indispensable needs of man. He wants to avoid imposing on man the cruel amputation, the inhuman experience, the steely lucidity that has been his own lot and the object of his dedication. What the Inquisitor denies by his own life, that is precisely what he must most strongly assert and raise up before man, as in a monstrance toward which man can stretch an adoring hand. For the spiritual goods that this monstrance contains are also goods that can be directly consumed.

Here is where the greatest difficulty arises, for the drive toward the Wholly Other is never fully complete, and this fact is a source of great potential danger. It leaves man unsatisfied; it gives rise to the most violent hopes and most unrestrained revolts; it disturbs the very depths of man. As soon as man reaches out his hand to something beyond the circle of his daily life, he calls everything into question; then he is quite capable of rejecting with scorn the bread so generously given to him. In the name of what? An illusion, a certainty—what difference does it make? The important thing is that such profound interior upheavals throw man off balance and drive him mad. The important thing, therefore, is to save man from himself.

Here is where the Master's genius is most fully revealed. The very thing that led man to raise challenging questions has now become the strongest support of the system; what created challenges now justifies; the impossible tension toward the Wholly Other becomes an adorable presence to a creature filled by this exquisite fruit; torturing absence turns into crystal-clear reality. Revelation in Christ turned upside down by Christianity; the revolution represented by freedom integrated into the state; religion incorporated into the system by the very one who denies religion: the need was to turn what was most dangerous and contradictory into something useful (a delicate task that meant handling material more powerful and unstable than nitroglycerine). The result? This object, with its meaning perverted and its power drained away, yet remaining itself, has at last been integrated into the whole, for the greater good of man, who can now advance peacefully toward his omega point. Everything is in harmony; all the pieces of the puzzle that is man are now in their proper place. Everything now fits together, and, since this means progress, we know for sure that we are on an ascending journey.

But was it not perverse cruelty to make things so difficult for man by confronting him with such antiquated, out-of-date choices as happiness or freedom, progress or truth? We know, after all, that it was only helplessness that forced man to make such choices.

Because man could not attain happiness, he pretended that he was free. Because he did not know his own power to make progress, he found his strength in clinging to the truth. But today we have transcended such limitations, rejected such alternatives. We see now that there is a straight, simple, well-marked road to follow; that happiness brings freedom, and that the advance of history inevitably leads us to the truth. And because we have learned the power of images, representations, symbols, and signifiers, we are now able to guarantee what man has never accomplished in the past. For if you take such values as justice, freedom, and truth—values which no philosopher or theologian has ever been able to define, values whose meaning and content such thinkers have never been able to explicate, but which nonetheless are rooted in this being, man, who is alienated from himself, and which if no one has been able to know, neither has anyone been able to destroy —is it not enough that man should *believe* he possesses them? What are they, after all, if no one experiences them? But if they are experienced, is that not enough? Is there any need to ask further questions about them? And what is the criterion for experiencing them? What measure must freedom attain? What constancy must virtue manifest? What obviousness must attach to justice?

For a long time we have known that these eternal things last but a fleeting moment. More important still, we know that it is all subjective. Where can I fix the dividing line between the true prophet and the false? Between the ecstasy that is from God and the madness of the mystic? Between the personal possession of freedom and the illusion of a free life that the psychotic in his straitjacket has? "These men are more convinced than ever that they are absolutely free," says the Grand Inquisitor. That is what really matters, is it not: that man should have a sense that justice is being done, that he is free, that the regime is truthful? that man should be possessed by these images and representations, which he uses as his spectacles for viewing reality? What else could he want? What other experience is there for him to have? These signifiers are real, even if there be nothing for them to signify.

"I could be bounded in a nutshell and count myself a king of infinite space."[17] So spoke the Prince of Denmark as he reflected on his own condition. Now it is the Grand Inquisitor who, for our good, causes us to feel that way a bit more each day, though we do not realize that he is thus changing our outlook. Thus, by an odd reversal, the same Grand Inquisitor, the realist who was so well able to discredit the word and make bread the important thing, and who managed easily to eliminate from the mainstream of history those who had only their poor verbiage to offer as compared with the effective raising of the living standard—this same Grand Inquisitor has now been forced by circumstances to become in his turn a master illusionist! The very person who had earlier denounced and laid bare all illusions.

The great difference, of course, is that the illusion he creates comes after he has filled men's hands, whereas previously, when confronted by the beggar's empty hands, the apostle could do nothing but proclaim the forgiveness of sins. We cannot but think that, when all is said and done, the illusion created in former times was a real deception, because it turned men aside from concrete, palpable, countable, measurable deeds. With the latter no error is possible: so many tons of steel, so many liters of acid. The illusion that the Grand Inquisitor propagates refers, on the contrary, to something so vague, uncertain, inexpressible, that no one can say whether or not it exists. But if such be its nature, can we call it any longer an illusion? Is it not, rather, reality itself? And is it not better for man to experience this vaporous simulacrum of freedom than to be plagued by cruel uncertainty about the real thing?

Of old, men sought a spiritual reality whose existence they did not doubt and to which they sacrificed everything material. But the radical questioning of all man's achievements undermined his great projects, and Babel was collapsing in ruins. Now, however, everything is splendidly in its precise place: the material order has attained its goal. Every aspiration to happiness is now satisfied through the accumulation of things, and the latter, ever more numerous, varied, and demanding of attention, are enlarging and reifying our world. The material world is at last receiving its proper status, while the spiritual is likewise being fulfilled, although in the form of experienced illusion. The spiritual world, too, is now in its proper place; it is a servant, playing the only role man can allow it to have. It is no longer an obstacle, no longer a distraction. Rather, it absorbs into itself any dangers that man's uncertainties and openness might still leave in him. The spiritual now need only be an illusion (since its object is utterly uncertain), but an illusion that must be experienced if it is fully to satisfy man's irrepressible need for it.

Does anything in all this still leave us uneasy? Do we find ourselves uncomfortable at the thought of so much paternalism on the part of him who seeks to bring man total happiness? Do we have the impression that man is being treated as a child? Do we suspect that relentless mechanisms are at work, operated by the technicians or the state, of which we may be ignorant? Traditional images of the sorcerer's apprentice haunt our minds. They make us uneasy, because the very existence of the images says that that sort of thing is indeed possible; at the same time, they reassure us, because after all the images are simply part of a well-known legend.

We can rest easy: the Grand Inquisitor is a man, just like

other men. He is master of all and runs the apparatus, but he is a man. We often think: "What man has built he will be able to run." That gives you the answer you want, does it not? Man has lost nothing and risks nothing: the Grand Inquisitor is a man, and therefore man is safe. I can be at peace; I have not lost the game. I can place my dignity, my maturity, my independence in the hands of those who know, those who have the threads of the tapestry in their hands and know just which buttons to push. I have my modest place in the system, for, after all, am I not one of them? I am part of a single system that conditions all its parts, but am I not in turn someone else's inquisitor?

Nonetheless, I am not the Grand Inquisitor, and as the parable ends I cannot but ask a final question: Who is the Grand Inquisitor? Our problem here is that we always think of the dark tragedy of the Spanish Inquisition, and we cannot help imagining dungeons and tortures. When we do so, we are tempted to say: Now that Hitler and Stalin are dead, no one in our world is the Grand Inquisitor. No one can now absorb into his sole person the complexity called for by the great adventure. Hitler and Stalin, like the Spanish Inquisition, were historical sports; any effort now to be a Grand Inquisitor would be a mere exercise in style.

It seems to me that, instead of saying that no one is the Grand Inquisitor now, it would be far better to say that the Grand Inquisitor is no one. When we put it that way, we get an insight into the reality of the Grand Inquisitor. In Ivan Karamazov's story, we see the bloodless, withered face of a nonagenarian. We forget one detail, however: in fact the Grand Inquisitor always kept his face veiled. No one must be allowed to recognize him; even the other inquisitors did not know each other's faces and persons. This rule was meant to ensure that their decisions would be objective, uninfluenced by outside pressures and hatred directed at them personally. It was meant to render the defense of truth and the exercise of justice completely impersonal. If power were to be full and complete and not tailored to any man's measure, it had to be anonymous.

Machiavelli's Prince and all the tyrants have human faces; that is why men can hate or love them. It is also why people can revolt and react against the visible, manifest oppression one individual exercises toward another. It is also why the tyrant relies on ill-founded calculations and yields to such human weaknesses as pride, fear, and death. The Grand Inquisitor, however, is faceless. His person eludes every grasp, for he is composed in fact of ten or a thousand individuals, all of them strangers and each of them part of a whole that we never know, but to which, however, we devote ourselves wholeheartedly.

This is why the Grand Inquisitor can be, in his total reality (not in this or that person), perfect justice and complete abnegation: love without weakness, skepticism without contempt. It is also why man can feel so free over against the Grand Inquisitor. The latter has no face to hate, no concrete being on which the curses of the wretched might fall. The individual has no embodied cruelty that he can denounce, no single will that is constraining his own. Wherever he goes, there is only an anonymous hand to guide his steps for his own greater good. All around is a coherent whole; it is there for his personal happiness and fulfillment and provides him with flexible, benevolent protection.

At the same time, the walls of his cell draw further apart as he advances, and when he finally manages to touch one of them, he finds it fully padded. Man still needs to feel and vent anger, and so they very kindly furnish him with some small secondary objects of no value on which he can exercise his self-justifying indignation and his phantom freedom. That is how we deal with children: we calm them down by giving them some old chinaware off the scrap heap to break.

Slowly the great whole gets organized. Each individual contributes his constructive individuality, his inventiveness, his good will, his love of others, and his passion for justice. The Grand Inquisitor can use everything as a means to his end. What he is and what he gives is what we make him be and what we give him first. He is simply the order (essential order; order as such) that unifies and integrates the sum of our dreams and desires: order as seen in the blinding light of motives evidently good; an order that no individual creates but that comes into existence through the contributions of each individual. Its nature, being order, is to introduce order into what are disparate shams, incoherent participations, and muddle-headed good wills.

Thus it is that after the bloodless planning and the reductive rationalizations everything falls into place by a process of growth that cannot be called spontaneous, since it is the result of calculation (but who does the calculating?). The growth is like the blind growth of a root that makes its way inexorably toward what nourishes it: a growth that is blind, yet guided. In the presence of this reality, which is perhaps the deepest of our age, we must walk with sacred reverence, advancing only on tiptoe. Let no man of the spirit disturb this growth whence man draws all he needs, which works entirely for the greatest good and happiness of this man. The man that you are; the man that I am.

"Why did you come to meddle with us, you with your questions! What right have you?"

Who would dare stand forth?

THOSE WHOM GOD WISHES TO DESTROY, HE FIRST MAKES MAD

I love the West, despite its vices and crimes. I love the vision of the prophets and the grace of the Parthenon, Roman order and the cathedrals, reason and the passionate longing for freedom. I love the perfection of western rural landscapes, the measure inherent in all it has produced, the great goals it has set itself. I love the West.

There is no need to remind me of the mines at Laurium and the crucifixion of slaves, the massacres of the Aztecs and the stake of the Inquisition. I know all about them, but I also know that, despite all those things, the history of the West is not a history of unrelieved criminality, and that what the West has given to the world weighs infinitely more in the scales than what it has done to societies and individuals. But there is no use talking about it. Writing this book has given me once again the feeling that I have done something absolutely useless, because no one will be able to accept it. No one in the West is able any longer to believe in the special vocation and special greatness of the western world.

We are caught up by a kind of doom from which, it seems, nothing can rescue us, for even the disciples of Christ are rushing headlong to destruction. Only the rejection of everything western, of everything the West has produced, can now satisfy the very men of the West. Throughout Europe and America we are watching a kind of mystery unfold; we are swept along in a vast procession of flagellants who slash at each other and themselves with the most horrendous of whips. We have donned disguises so that no one may be able to recognize the virtues of the men and women of our world. We have smeared ourselves with paint and blood to show our contempt for all that created the great civilization from which we spring. We even scourge ourselves hysterically for crimes we did not commit! In short, we show enthusiastic joy only at what denies, destroys, and degrades all the works of the West. We trample on the body of the West and spit in its face.

If the nineteenth century betrayed the West by having a good conscience (this never reflected the true attitude of the West), we are betraying it by our bad conscience, which has now turned into insanity. Look back over the films of the last twenty years, and you will see to your amazement that the only successful ones have been those that have broadcast scorn for the West, filth, and self-scourging. No argument has any value in the face of evidence like that, of such commonplaces accepted without a murmur. Reason is useless, as is any process of self-awareness. The only "truth" people are willing to "become aware of" is the shameful condition of the western world.

I see Europe marching with giant steps to its end: not for economic or technical or political reasons, not because it is being overwhelmed by the third world (which is in fact impotent), not because it is also being challenged by China, but simply because it has decided to commit suicide. All the behavior (and I mean literally all of it) of the technicians, the bureaucrats, the politicians, and, at bottom (despite appearances), the philosophers, the film-makers, and the scientists is suicidal. Everything of a positive character that may be found is immediately turned inside out, distorted, and stood on its head so as to become a new source of accusation or a new means of destruction. The Left has triumphantly joined the Right in this race toward death, while Christianity celebrates its marriage with Marxism and proceeds to slay the old, impotent flesh that was once the glory of the world.

In this agreement of opposites on this single point I cannot see a natural response to a situation or a spontaneous development. The very fact that the strongest arguments, the most rigorous demonstrations, the clearest dangers, the most tested values, and the most scientifically grounded certainties are of no avail, and that nothing can influence in the slightest way the determination of the technicians or the discourses of the pseudo-revolutionaries, is proof that we are faced with something of a quite different kind. When we run up against that kind of unanimity and inflexibility, we are not dealing with a conscious decision clearly made in the light of thorough knowledge. No, the rejection of the dialectical process that has been the lifeblood of the West, the total blindess to the risk of failure, and the destructive rage that marks it all are due to what some have called destiny or fate, others Jupiter or nemesis.

In any case, some god is blinding men. Despite the choices still possible and the options still available, despite the paths still open to be taken, despite the warnings of prophets and sentries, despite the outcries of the poets and the weak, this blindness is now leading men to will, at any cost, their own destruction. With their own hands they are tearing down their citadels and turning reason into unreason.

In this overall process, I think three movements can be seen. A brief description of these will be my final word in this book, the final (useless) analysis I can offer before the mad conflagration is upon us.

The first movement is that of *blind negation,* a retreat into unqualified negation of all the West has been and can yet be. Some of its embodiments: the frenzied pleasure in destroying and rejecting, in playing the man without a future or the artist without culture; the sadism of the intellectual who tears language—his own language—to pieces, and who does not want to say anything further, because in fact there is nothing to say;

the explosion of words, because there is no more communication; the mockeries that are regarded as works of art; and finally, the suicides, physical among the young, intellectual or in the area of creativity among the writers, painters, and musicians. All this is happening because these people regard the "system" as utterly frightful, and see it as immediately absorbing and rationalizing every project whatsoever. They feel caught by an inescapable dilemma, since even their irrationalities serve as compensation for the system and thus become part of it (although it never becomes clear in what precisely the famous "system" consists).

In order to avoid this kind of absorption by the system, it is found necessary to radicalize endlessly all positions, all projects, all oppositions. But in radicalizing in this obsessive manner, all these people are effectively destroying, first and foremost, the very thing they should be saving and preserving: the fragile remnants of what is authentic in our world and our time, the things that should be carefully preserved as a possible starting point for a whole new hope.

Because morality has become valueless and evidence of sheer hypocrisy, men reject even the things that could have been the threatened seed of an ethical renewal, but a renewal that is now no longer desired. Morality was the prerogative of the bourgeoisie, and therefore everything smacking of morality is rejected. No one seems to realize that there has never been a society without a moral code, and that the chief thing lacking in our western world is precisely an ethical code and a system of accepted values. As soon as there is even a tiny blossoming of values, the intellectuals rise up to reject it and jeer at it. In doing so, they give no proof that they are free and intelligent, but demonstrate only that they are impotent and have surrendered to the madness in which negation becomes an end in itself.

What we are seeing today is not simply obedience to the celebrated advice "The first duty is to say No." I have used that statement as an epigraph for some of my books, and I meant what it says: the *first* duty, which implies a second. Today, however, like stupid oxen that slowly shake their heads from side to side, the intellectuals and the artists are capable only of the No; beyond that there is nothing—except the void that is their work. Fragmentary theater and deciphered Molière, poetry without words and music that is sheer noise, destructured language, Lacan, Derrida, and all their second-rate imitators who think that absolute incomprehensibility offers a way out, when in fact we have shut the door on all possibilities and hopes, and have sunk into a resignation that knows no future. There is no longer anything to live for: that is what these intellectuals are saying without realizing it; the blinding light they shed is that of a sun on the point of sinking into the sea. Virtuosity has never been a substitute for truth. Withdrawal into virtuosity of this kind shows only that for these intellectuals, the last Cardinal Eminences of the western world, there is no longer any such thing as truth.

The second of the three movements may simply be called *movement without direction*. Over thirty years ago, I wrote in my book *The Presence of the Kingdom*[1] that we are rushing nowhere at an ever increasing speed. The western world is moving rapidly, and ever more so, but there is no orbit for it to take up, no point toward which it is heading, no place, no goal. We see the mistakes we have made, but we continue to make them with an apparently blind obstinacy. We know that there is an atomic threat and what it means, but like moles we go on building H-bombs and atomic energy plants. We know the implications of pollution, but we go on calmly polluting the air, the rivers, and the ocean. We know men are going mad from living in huge conglomerations, but we, like automatons, go on building them. We know the dangers of pesticides and chemical fertilizers, but we continue to use them in increasingly massive doses. We know all this, but we are like the masochist who knows others have put a little arsenic in each bowl of soup he drinks, but who goes on drinking it day after day, as though impelled by a force he cannot resist.

Our speed is constantly increasing, and it does not matter whither we are going. We are caught up in the madness and hybris of the dance of death: the important thing is the dance, the saturnalia, the bacchanalia, the lupercalia. We are no longer worried about what will emerge from it or about the void to which it points. We are content to die of dancing. Our generation is not even capable of cynicism. It takes a kind of terrible greatness to say, "After me, the deluge." No one says that today; on the contrary, everyone is glutted with promises and regards the mad dance as a way to authentic renewal. Yet there is no goal, nothing transcendent, no value to light the way; the movement is enough.

In the churches, the preaching of the Word is replaced by the flutterings of ecstasy, and when someone falls into a trance, that is regarded as proof of spiritual authenticity. The intellectuals caught up in this directionless movement take the lids off bottomless wells; they lean over them and fall in. Hermeneutics—the interpretation of interpretations—is symbolic of this frenzied intellectual agitation, this increasing refinement of a type of thinking that, given its premises, cannot possibly lead anywhere.

The individual thinker is immured in his own little area; he is unwilling to listen to what others say or to heed their interruptions and warnings. Schools and projects are here today and gone tomorrow; thousands of books are published each year, all the more brilliant in proportion as they contain and say less; tomorrow there will be not a trace left of them. The important thing is movement for movement's sake. We have already seen that sort of thing in politics: "Socialism is the movement, not the goal." Therefore, do not look at what socialism has actually accomplished in the Soviet Union or elsewhere. Look only at our manifestos and struggles, our preparations for the revolution (a "revolution" toward nothing, toward an alternative never defined), our denunciations of evil. Look at our vigorous activity; be satisfied with that, and come with us.

The nihilistic revolution has succeeded. Today's political activists who still claim to be revolutionaries have nothing to put in nihilism's place. Movement for movement's sake, thorough study for the study's sake, the revolution for the revolution's sake: that, they say, is the only way to escape the system. It is a remarkable thing, however, that this system renders mad not only those who are part of it but those who reject it as well. The system is now the god who makes men mad, but it is a god we have created with our own minds.

The third of the three movements is that of *repetitiveness within the acceleration.* Not only are we caught up in the accelerating movements, not only are history and the spread of information and scientific discovery and population statistics and productivity accelerating without purpose or meaning, as we just indicated, but the acceleration is also characterized by a vast repetitiveness and redundancy. If by some extraordinary chance a new idea appears (a new idea, not a new thought: there are no new thoughts, just as there is neither understanding nor authenticity), a thousand books are immediately written to repeat it—provided, of course, the new idea is conformist and fits in with the effort to tear everything apart.

We live in a world of limitless repetition, which we like to believe is inventiveness, novelty, a constant new beginning. In our ignorance we imagine that by aping the exact sciences and their rational methods we are thinking and experiencing ever more deeply and fully. Yet once we strip away the illusionist's veil of pseudo-scientific language or the layer of obscurity caused by a fragmented discourse, and look at what our sociologists, psychologists, psychoanalysts, Marxists, historians (yes, history too is now dedicated to obscurity), novelists, and poets are trying to say, we are appalled at the emptiness, inanity, and incoherence of their thought. We realize that there is only a vast repetitiveness. Everything they say is completely familiar and has long since become commonplace.

This inability to innovate except by ringing the changes on signs (not symbols) is for me a proof that the end of the West is upon us: the end of reason, the end of self-awareness and self-criticism, the end of freedom, the end of the individual. I know, of course, that those whom I am attacking (and who will never read what I say) will jauntily shrug their shoulders and say, "None of that means anything to us. Reason and the rest of it are just cultural inventions that have no objective reality. As for the West, what is the West to us? We are no one's sons." I would rephrase the final statement: We are nothing, sons of no one. We are but the repetition of a fading echo, a mere movement of Brownian particles that do not exist as such and are discernible only by the track they leave for a thousandth of a second before vanishing.

Those now responsible for the heritage of the West bluster and say it is no business of theirs. Well, the West cannot live on nothing. The politicians and the economists will not keep it alive. The astonishingly deep and balanced creation I have tried to bring before the reader in this book is now close to its end, simply through the fault of those who did not understand it and were incapable of grasping it. I am speaking of all the intellectuals. I mean *all* of them without a single exception: all those who have a reputation and do the talking, the men who create the myths. Today it is the myths of death, and they alone, that speak to us in our madness. The West is at its end —but that does not necessarily mean the end of the world.

NOTES

Prologue

[1][Rutilius Claudius Namatianus was a Latin poet of the fifth century A.D. In 416 he returned to Gaul after spending some time in Rome, and described his homeward journey in a poem *De reditu suo* (On His Return).—Tr.]

Chapter I

[1]["Story of the Centuries" is an allusion to Victor Hugo's *Légende des siècles,* three series of epic poems (1859, 1877, 1893), in which scenes from different periods depict the historical and spiritual development of mankind.—Tr.]

[2][Béhanzin was the name of a nineteenth-century king of Dahomey, who became well-known for his cruelty.—Tr.]

[3]["Time has turned on its fragile heel" is a variation of a line from a poem by Aragon, *La valse d'Elsa.* The line itself is quoted below in Chapter 3.—Tr.]

[4][*Transitio ad plebem* or "crossing over to the people" was a juridical act by which a Roman patrician became a plebeian, so that he could take part in the assembly of the plebs and possibly become a tribune of the plebs.—Tr.]

[5]["Nessus' shirt": In Greek mythology, the centaur Nessus, fatally wounded by Heracles, persuaded Heracles' wife, Deianira, to take and keep a portion of his, Nessus', blood as a charm to preserve her

husband's love. Later on, Deianira steeped a robe of Heracles' in the blood, thinking thereby to keep him faithful to her. The poison penetrated the hero's body, and the robe stuck to his skin, so that to remove it he had to tear away pieces of his flesh.—Tr.]

[6]["Anti-Cartierist": "Cartierism" was a view advanced by a well-known French journalist, Cartier, at the time of decolonization; he argued that France should refuse to help the former colonies.—Tr.]

[7][Maxime Rodinson: contemporary French islamologist. Several of his books have been translated into English: *Islam and the Arabs* (translated by Michael Perl; New York, 1968); *Mohammed* (translated by Anne Carter; New York, 1971); *Islam and Capitalism* (translated by Bryan Pearce; New York, 1973).—Tr.]

[8][Monségur: Chief city of the Albigensians, captured by the French armies in 1244.—Tr.]

[9][Three important medieval Arab philosophers: Averroes (Ibn Rushd), 1126–1198; Avicenna (Ibn Sina), 980–1037; Alkindi (Abu-Yusuf Ya'Qub Ibn Ishaq al-Kindi), d. ca. 900.—Tr.]

[10][Qurban Said: fourteenth-century Muslim theologian.—Tr.]

[11][Colonel Qaddafi: Colonel Muammar el-Qaddafi, Prime Minister of Libya since the overthrow of the monarchy in 1969.—Tr.]

[12][Jean Genet: Contemporary French novelist and dramatist.—Tr.]

[13][Papillon: Henri Charrière, former convict who wrote his memoirs in a book entitled *Papillon;* the book enjoyed an enormous success in France (1970).—Tr.]

[14][Georges Bataille: Contemporary French philosopher with ties to the surrealists; introduced the idea of the "consumer society." One of his books has been translated into English: *Eroticism* (translated by Mary Dalwood; London, 1962).—Tr.]

[15]Translated by Patricia Wolf (New York, 1971).

[16]I am well aware that the whole study of myth by the historians is opposed to what I am saying here, and that the work of Paul Veyne (for example) on method in history is excellent. Nor am I hostile to all quantitative history: the works of Fernand Braudel and Pierre Chaunu are very successful and stand as models of the genre. But these tendencies and successes do not change the fact that the vast majority of historians are scientistic, positivist, shallowly rationalistic, and overspecialized.

[17][Antonin Artaud (1896–1948): Poet, dramatist, actor, and theoretician of the surrealist movement.—Tr.]

[18][Jacques Lacan: Contemporary French theoretician of psychoanalysis.—Tr.]

[19][Philippe Sollers: Contemporary French novelist and critic.—Tr.]

[20][Michel Foucault: Contemporary French sociologist and historian.—Tr.]

[21]Erich Auerbach, *Mimesis: The Representation of Reality in Western*

Literature (translated by Willard Trask; Princeton, N.J., 1953).

[22]Konrad Lorenz, *On Aggression* (translated by Marjorie Kerr Wilson; New York, 1966).

[23]Norbert Elias has given a description of this in his *La civilisation des moeurs* (Paris, 1973). The book is clearly of interest and rich in historical detail. Its starting point, however, is the presupposition that to the extent that we restrain an impulse, to that extent we depart from "man." Such a position is diametrically opposed to the one I am adopting here.

[24]Cf. my book *Propaganda: The Formation of Men's Attitudes* (translated by Ronald Kellen and Jean Lerner; New York, 1965). I am preparing a book of word and image that will appear shortly.

[25][Johnny Halliday: A pop singer who was very well known in France.—Tr.]

[26]Here, of course, I am using the language current in the trends I am criticizing. One would have to prove that there is such a thing as "human nature," and to show what it is, before one could define anything as being "anti-natural." The groups in question, however, have no interest in defining anything whatsoever!

[27]Michel Foucault, *Madness and Civilization: A History of Madness in the Age of Reason* (translated by Richard Howard; New York, 1965).

[28]As I have shown in my *Métamorphose du bourgeois* (Paris, 1967).

[29][Wilhelm Reich (1897–1957): Austrian-born psychiatrist and social critic; promulgated theories about "orgone energy" which is supposedly found in the atmosphere and in living organisms, and is capable of being concentrated in various ways, including the use of an "orgone accumulator."—Tr.]

[30]Translated by C. Edward Hopkin (New York, 1973).

[31]Anders Nygren, *Eros and Agape* (translated by Philip S. Watson; Philadelphia, 1963).

[32][The phrase "sickness of the West" is from Henri Massis. Cf., in English, his *Defense of the West* (translated by F. S. Flint; London, 1927).—Tr.]

[33]When we compare the resurrection of Christ with that of the gods (Attis and others) who were reborn, and when we say that these religions (not all of them, since the most important of them remained outside the empire) created a climate favorable to the new religion because they were spread throughout the empire, we must bear in mind that all these religions came from the East, frequently from beyond the frontiers, and were purer in form in their homeland than they were at Rome.

[34]Cf. on this subject the excellent book by Jean Brun, *Le retour de Dionysos* (Paris, 1969).

[35]It should have become clear by the end of this analysis that when I speak of the two faces of the West, I am not at all taking the same

position as Maurice Duverger in his *Janus: Les deux faces de l'Occident* (Paris, 1972). Duverger's thesis is fairly well known: one face of the West is liberalism, which reached its climactic form in liberal democracy, and the other is capitalism and technicity, which together produce a techno-democracy. We may observe that when he analyzes the latter, he is content to reproduce what I wrote in 1950 on the effects of technicity on democracy, and in 1960 on the effects of propaganda on democracy, although in those days he was quite hostile to the ideas he has now adopted. But when he claims to be describing the *basic contradiction* of the West—a contradiction inherent in techno-democracy and consisting in an increase in productivity and consumption but a decrease in the quality of life; a contradiction between the expansion and simultaneous degradation of the conditions of human existence—he remains at a level of triviality and superficiality that the West surely does not deserve. The contradiction to which the West is subject is much more fundamental and long-standing (since the whole development of the West is based on it) and at the same time is constitutive of the very greatness and progress of the West. This contradiction may even be said to *be* the West!

Chapter II

[1][Adolphe Thiers (1797–1877): Statesman, journalist, historian, and first president of the Third Republic. Charles Maurras (1868–1952): Writer and political theorist; founded the review (later a daily newspaper), *L'Action française,* organ of the royalist party.—Tr.]

[2][The maxim in this form is from Publilius Syrus, first century A.D., but the sentiment has been repeated in various forms down the centuries.—Tr.]

[3]I have to laugh at the eminent sociologists working in the field of communications who solemnly decided in 1974 that "the star system has disappeared"!

[4][Gisèle Halimi: Parisian lawyer of the extreme Left, well known for her stands in behalf of sexual freedom and feminism.—Tr.]

[5][Abbé Pierre (H.-A. Grouès-Pierre): French priest, founder of the Emmaus Community. Cf. Boris Simon, *Abbé Pierre and the Ragpickers of Emmaus* (translated by Lucie Noel; New York, 1955).—Tr.]

[6]Guy Sajer writes the tragic story of such a fate in his novel *The Forgotten Soldier* (translated by Lily Emmet; New York, 1971).

[7]This passage was written in January, 1974.

[8]I wrote the preceding pages on the Arab governments in January, 1974, and prefer now to leave them unchanged.

[9][Henri Béraud: French journalist of the nineteen-thirties who wrote several important reports on the rise of fascism and Nazism. Madame Irene Joliot-Curie (1870–1956): Physicist, daughter of

Pierre and Marie Curie. Simone de Beauvoir: Contemporary French novelist and essayist.—Tr.]

[10]*Le Monde,* April 15–19, 1974.

[11]I must insist that I am not saying this because I was in favor of a French Algeria. As a matter of fact, I was in favor of decolonization and independence at least as far back as 1935–36 after the *Rapport Violette* and the *Voyage au Congo.*

[12]It is quite interesting to read now the articles written at the time of the Kravchenko affair.

[13]A. Fontaine has a fine article on the Kurds in *Le Monde* for March 19, 1975, but it amounts to an obituary on this people.

[14][Alain Peyreffitte: New French Minister of Justice.—Tr.]

[15][L. Makhno: Ukrainian anarchist and skilled guerilla fighter in ca. 1919.—Tr.]

[16][Spartacists: A revolutionary socialist group (World War I) that became the nucleus of the German Communist Party. Rosa Luxemburg (1871–1919): A revolutionary theoretician and activist, founder of the Spartacus League; murdered during the civil strife after World War I.—Tr.]

[17][Monatte: French trade-unionist leader.—Tr.]

[18]The leftist propagandists with their simplistic interpretations of everything are incapable of recognizing this indisputable historical fact. They deny that the vast majority of black slaves were satisfied with their lot and even loved their masters. Yet the blacks proved this when the War of Secession broke out. The official truth, on the Left, is that the whip was the only bond between master and slave; that the slaves all lived in terror; that there were countless runaways, ravenous dogs were everywhere, and Tyler with his handful of men was representative of all the slaves. But that whole picture is pure imagination, dreamed up because it matches what today's leftist intellectuals believe to be the dialectic of history!

[19]For clarity's sake I must repeat that I am thus indicting the Left only because the Left was, in my view, the sole legitimate heir of the West and contained in itself the promise of the world's future. My attack is not intended as a rehabilitation of the Right or a plea on its behalf. Let me say it again: In my view the Right has no future, no legitimacy, no existence. I have nothing in common with the Right, and if those of the Right speak as I do, it is because they misunderstand me. I am well aware that with its usual simplistic conformism the Left will say, "If you criticize the Left, you must belong to the Right," or "By speaking as you do, you supply the Right with ammunition." That kind of thinking is childish. The real point I am making is that, now that the Left has betrayed the West, there is nothing left. Western history is finished.

[20]Another caution: In writing this I evidently have no intention of

saying that the poor should remain subject to the domination, dictatorship, and violence of others. I am saying only that the poor man should be the living rejection of all power. The domination of one class should not be replaced by the domination of another, but all domination should be rejected and, if nothing else will serve, be destroyed.

[21]Cf. *Autopsy of Revolution* (translated by Patricia Wolf; New York, 1971), and *De la révolution aux révoltes* (Paris, 1972).

[22]Cf. Roland Mousnier, *Peasant Uprisings in Seventeenth Century France* (translated by Bryan Pearce; New York, 1970).

[23]This is also why it is that, when using a schema for revolution that is correlated with an abstract reality, people are forced to fall back on simplistic images, such as the cigar-smoking capitalist; the images stir basic feelings of rebellion, but lead revolutionary action in an entirely wrong direction.

[24]Edgar Morin, *Le paradigme humain* (Paris, 1972); Georges Friedmann, *La puissance et la sagesse* (Paris, 1970); Bertrand de Jouvenel, *Arcadie: Essais sur le mieux-vivre* (Paris, 1968); Ivan Illich, *Tools for Conviviality* (New York, 1973); Radovan Richta, *Civilization at the Crossroads: Social and Human Implications of the Scientific and Technological Revolution* (3rd.ed.; translated by Marian Slingová; White Plains, N.Y., 1969).

[25]It is worth noting that just this year (1975) the French Left is proclaiming itself in favor of the consumer society!

[26][Louis Althusser: Contemporary French Marxist philosopher. Cf., in English, his *For Marx* (translated by Ben Brewster; New York, 1969) and, with Etienne Balibar, *Reading Capital* (translated by Ben Brewster; New York, 1970).—Tr.]

Chapter III

[1]Karl Mannheim is still referred to as having been one of the first to raise the problem of utopianism, in his *Ideology and Utopia: An Introduction to the Sociology of Knowledge* (translated by Louis Wirth and Edward Shils; New York, 1936; German original, 1929). We should recall, however, that Lewis Mumford was the first to write a history, and a good one, of utopias, in 1927: *The Story of Utopias* (New York, 1927). In this book he clearly raised all the problems that have since been discussed.

[2]I have already attacked utopianism in two earlier books, but from viewpoints that are different from the one I am taking here. Utopianism seems to me to be at present one of the major ideological dangers. Many books have been written about this danger, from Karl Mannheim down to Gilles Lapouge (*Utopie et civilisation* [Paris, 1973]) by way of Henri Lefebvre (*La somme et le reste* [Paris, 1956]) and Jean

Servier (*Histoire de l'utopie* [Paris, 1971]). In these pages I shall, however, refer chiefly to the excellent and overlooked book of François Laplantine, *Les trois voix de l'imaginaire: Le messianisme, la possession, et l'utopie. Etude ethnopsychiatrique* (Paris, 1974).

[3][Charles Fourier (1772–1837): French social philosopher. His utopia was organized in small economic units, called "phalanxes," of 1620 individuals. His teaching spread to America, where it influenced Brook Farm for a while.—Tr.]

[4]This and all the following quotations are from Laplantine's book.

[5]Cf. his *Le droit à la paresse.*

[6]Poor China of Mao, on its way to such a utopia as this!

[7][Etienne Cabet (1788–1856): French utopian reformer. His ideal society was described in his *Voyage en Icarie* (1840), and the members of his several communistic settlements in the United States were called Icarians.—Tr.]

[8]Here I am using the word "bourgeois" in the sense I gave it in my *Métamorphose du bourgeois* (Paris, 1967).

[9]Cf. Yona Friedmann, *L'Architecture mobile: Vers une cité conçue par ses habitants* (Tournai, 1970) and *Pour une architecture scientifique* (Paris, 1971). Ernst Bloch, *A Philosophy of the Future* (translated by John Cumming; New York, 1970). Henri Lefebvre, *L'Espace urbain* (Paris, 1976).

[10]Cf. his *Sociologie de l'utopie* (Paris, 1961).

[11]This is the popular slogan. I have elsewhere shown what its objective content amounts to, once it is analyzed.

[12][The Châtelet—"little castle"—was an ancient prison in Paris.—Tr.]

[13][A line from Aragon's poem, *La valse d'Elsa.*—Tr.]

[14]["The Green Sun" was the title of a science fiction movie (1974) justifying cannibalism in a modern city.—Tr.]

[15][Massu was a French general who used torture in Algeria.—Tr.]

[16][The legend of the Grand Inquisitor appears in Dostoievsky's *The Brothers Karamazov,* Part II, Book 5, Chapter 5.—Tr.]

[17]*Hamlet,* Act II, Scene 2.

Epilogue

[1]Translated by Olive Wyon (London, 1951). The French original was published in 1948.